MW00884454

EFFECTIVE COMMUNICATION SKILLS FOR PERSONAL AND PROFESSIONAL SUCCESS

IMPROVING PERSONAL AND PROFESSIONAL RELATIONSHIPS WHILE OVERCOMING COMMUNICATION BARRIERS

DEREK CRUMMY

CONTENTS

INTRODUCTION

Effective communication is the cornerstone of both personal and professional success. Throughout my forty-plus years in financial services, I've witnessed firsthand the power of well-crafted communication: it can open doors to new opportunities and mend bridges that seemed permanently broken. Conversely, missed connections and misunderstandings cause needless conflict and lost opportunities. Whether sealing a complex financial deal or maintaining harmony at home with my partner of many years, the ability to convey thoughts clearly and receive messages accurately has made all the difference.

My name is Derek, and I've dedicated much of my career to navigating Ireland's intricate world of financial services. This extensive experience has ingrained in me the understanding that the principles of effective communication, whether in a boardroom or a personal setting, remain constant. This book is my sincere attempt to share these principles with you.

In this book, Effective Communication Skills for Personal and Professional Success, we will not only delve into communication theory but also bridge the gap between theory and practical application. My goal is to provide you with tools that are not just theoretical but also actionable, offering immediate benefits to enhance your daily interactions. This book is tailored for you, the career-focused and personal development-oriented individual eager to improve your interpersonal skills and professional relationships. It's designed to help you achieve your goals.

Why does this matter? Every interaction is an opportunity to build relationships, influence outcomes, and make an impact. Think about your current communication habits. Are they serving your personal and professional goals? Could they be improved? This book offers you the strategies I've learned and applied throughout my career, ensuring you're heard and genuinely understood.

This book is more than just another communication guide. It's a practical, experience-backed journey to improving your ability to connect with others effectively. Each chapter combines theory with real-world application, equipping you with the necessary success tools. From understanding the basics of communication and overcoming barriers to mastering personal relationships and professional interactions, each section concludes with key takeaways and actionable advice.

Are you ready to transform the way you communicate? This book is not just a guide; it's a transformative journey. Let's embark on this journey together. It's time to enhance your connections, achieve professional success, and engage in more meaningful interactions. Let's get started and unlock your full communication potential.

UNDERSTANDING COMMUNICATION BASICS

Have you ever considered how a simple 'hello' can make or break a first impression or how a well-timed joke can elevate a tense meeting? It's all part of the fascinating world of communication. This first chapter is your toolkit for understanding the nuts and bolts of how we communicate. We'll explore the psychological underpinnings of communication, why context matters, and how our brains can sometimes be our worst enemies in getting the message across. By the end of this chapter, you'll understand these concepts and start to see the invisible threads that connect every interaction you have.

1.1 THE PSYCHOLOGY BEHIND COMMUNICATION: UNLOCKING THE BASICS

Understanding Human Needs

At its core, communication is about fulfilling basic human needs. This understanding, rooted in our shared human experience, is crucial. From the dawn of time, humans have needed to share information, from warning about lurking predators to expressing feelings of love or fear. Today, though the sabre-toothed tigers might be replaced with boardroom battles, the fundamental need to connect with others remains unchanged. A renowned psychologist, Abraham Maslow, illustrated this in his famous hierarchy of needs. At the very foundation, we have physiological needs, followed by safety, but soon after comes love and belonging. This is where communication is key. Whether it's a heart-to-heart with a friend or a strategic email to colleagues, effective communication helps fulfil this deep-seated need for connection and belonging. It's not just about transmitting information; it's about connecting on a human level.

Influence of Perception

Let's talk about perception—our individual way of seeing the world. It shapes every interaction we have. For instance, if you've ever misread a text message from someone and thought they were being short with you, only to find out later they were just in a rush, you've experienced how perception influences communication. Our brains take shortcuts based on past experiences, societal norms, and personal biases, all colouring our interpretation of messages. This means that two people can interpret the same information differently. Being aware of this can help you tailor your communication in a way that minimises misunderstandings and maximises clarity. Remember, it's not just what you say; how, when, and why you say it can alter someone's perception.

The Power of Context

Context acts like the stage setting for your communication—it can dramatically change a message's meaning. Consider how a stern "We need to talk" feels in a cosy, private setting versus a public, noisy cafe. The words are the same, but the setting changes how you might perceive them. Context includes the physical setting and the cultural and emotional backdrop to any communication. For example, giving constructive feedback in a culture that values directness, like the United States, is different from doing so in a culture that values harmony, like Japan. Understanding and adapting to the context can prevent your message from losing its intended meaning and help ensure it is received as intended.

Cognitive Biases in Communication

Finally, let's tackle cognitive biases—those pesky mental shortcuts that can lead to judgment errors. Confirmation bias, for instance, is a common mental trap that causes people to seek information confirming their pre-existing beliefs and ignore information that contradicts them. This can be particularly detrimental in communication, as it might lead you to misinterpret what someone is saying simply because it doesn't align with your existing beliefs. By recognising and mitigating these biases, you can improve your understanding dramatically. It involves being open to new information and perspectives and questioning your assumptions. This not only makes you a better communicator but also a more empathetic and understanding human being, fostering a deeper connection with others.

In this section, we've just scratched the surface of the psychology behind communication, uncovering the basic elements that influence how we share and receive information. As we progress, keep these concepts in mind—they are the foundation for effective communication. Remember, the significance of clarifying messages to avoid miscommunication cannot be overstated. It's a crucial step that ensures your message is received as intended, fostering a sense of security and confidence in your communication skills.

1.2 VERBAL VS. NON-VERBAL: BALANCING THE SCALES OF EXPRESSION

When you think about communication, it's easy to prioritise the words we use—the verbal side of the equation. However, if you've ever watched a silent movie or observed a couple communicating with just glances across a crowded room, you know that non-verbal cues can speak volumes. In fact, experts suggest that a staggering percentage of our communication is non-verbal. This includes not only facial expressions and body language but also our voice's tone, pace, and volume. Imagine you're giving a presentation. The words are important, but how you say those words can dramatically change the message. Speak too quickly, and you might come across as nervous or unprepared; too slowly, you risk boring your audience or appearing unenthusiastic. The volume of your voice also plays a crucial role—too soft, and you're inaudible; too loud, and you might be seen as aggressive. Balancing these elements effectively ensures your verbal message delivers information and the right emotional tone and emphasis, making you more aware and in control of your communication.

Now, let's delve into the world of non-verbal communication. It's fascinating how our bodies can give away our true feelings, sometimes even contradicting our words. A furrowed brow, a quick eye roll, or an enthusiastic nod can tell you more about someone's response than their words. Decoding these cues requires keen observation and a bit of psychological understanding. For instance, crossed arms might indicate that someone is defensive or uncomfortable while mirroring your body language can suggest agreement and rapport. But here's a kicker—not all non-verbal cues are universal. What's considered polite or positive in one culture can be rude or negative in another. A thumbs-up, for instance, is positive in many Western cultures but can be offensive in parts of the Middle East and Asia.

This brings us to the crucial aspect of synchronising verbal and non-verbal communication. This synchronisation, where your words and body language align, is key. Consistency between what you say and how you say it builds trust and clarity in your message. Imagine telling a colleague you're open to their ideas while your body is turned away from them or saying you're fine when your tone is steeped in frustration. These mixed signals can confuse and even alienate your audience. On the flip side, when your words and body language align, your message becomes more powerful and believable. This synchronisation applies to individual interactions and plays a significant role in professional settings, where the stakes are often higher. The scope for misunderstanding can have real consequences.

Cultural variations in non-verbal communication are particularly intriguing. While a smile is universally recognised as a positive expression, the context in which it is used can vary widely. In some cultures, smiling too much can be seen as a sign of frivolity or a lack of seriousness. Similarly, the appropriate distance to maintain during a conversation can differ vastly. In some Southern European or Latin American cultures, standing close to someone while talking signifies warmth and friendliness.

In contrast, in Northern European and some Asian cultures, maintaining a larger personal space is preferred and considered respectful. Understanding these nuances is crucial, especially in today's globalised work environment, where interactions with people from diverse backgrounds are common. It helps avoid potential gaffes and builds smoother, more respectful personal and professional relationships.

In summary, mastering the art of communication is as much about the words you choose as it is about how you deliver them and the non-verbal messages you send. Whether modulating your voice or being mindful of your gestures, each aspect plays a pivotal role in ensuring your message is heard, understood, and received in the spirit it was intended. So, next time you're in a conversation, take a moment to notice what you say and how you say it. The results might just surprise you.

1.3 ACTIVE LISTENING: MORE THAN JUST HEARING

Unlike passive hearing, which most of us default to, active listening involves fully engaging with the speaker—processing, understanding, and responding thoughtfully to what's being said. Think about the last time you really listened to someone. Not just the passive nodding while your mind wanders to your grocery list, but truly focusing on their words, emotions, and non-verbal cues. That's active listening. It's an intentional act, requiring effort and focus. The goal isn't just to hear the words but to understand the complete message being conveyed.

So, what stops us from listening effectively? Several barriers can get in the way. Distractions are a major culprit—be it the ping of a smartphone or the chatter in a busy cafe. Then there's our own mental baggage. Sometimes, we listen not to understand but to reply, crafting our next comment instead of processing what's being said. Emotional biases also play a role; for instance, if someone has rubbed us the wrong way in the past, we might tune out their ideas or feedback. Overcoming these obstacles starts with awareness. Recognising when and why you're not listening is the first step toward better, more active engagement with others.

Improving your active listening skills can be transformative. Start by giving the speaker your full attention. This might mean silencing your phone, closing your laptop, or simply clearing your mind of distractions. Maintaining eye contact shows respect and interest and helps you stay focused. As you listen, don't just wait for your turn to speak. Process the information and think about the emotions and intentions behind the words. You can use techniques like paraphrasing what the speaker has said before adding your thoughts. It demonstrates that you've understood and allows the speaker to clarify if necessary. Asking open-ended questions also enriches the conversation and provides deeper insights into the speaker's thoughts and feelings.

The role of active listening in fostering empathy cannot be overstated. By truly listening, you connect with the speaker on a deeper level. You come to understand their perspectives and feelings, not just their words. This connection is essential for building trust and rapport in any relationship—be it with a spouse, a colleague, or even a stranger. People who feel heard are more open, honest, and cooperative. It's a feedback loop of positivity; as your empathetic listening helps others feel valued, your relationships deepen, enhancing your personal and professional life.

Active listening is more than a tool for effective communication; it demonstrates respect and care. It influences how you connect with people, understand their viewpoints, and respond to their needs. Whether you're negotiating a contract, resolving a conflict, or supporting a friend, how well you listen determines how well you relate to others. It's a skill that can be learned and improved upon and has profound effects. Embracing active listening is embracing a commitment to truly engage with the world around you, which enriches your interactions and overall life experience.

1.4 THE ROLE OF EMPATHY IN UNDERSTANDING AND BEING UNDERSTOOD

Empathy and sympathy are often invited to the same parties, but they're not quite best friends. They mingle with guests differently. Sympathy might pat you on the back while offering you a comforting nod, essentially feeling sorry for your troubles. On the other hand, empathy tries to put itself in your shoes, understanding your feelings and, perhaps, even sharing a tear. In communication, this distinction is crucial. Empathy involves a deeper connection, a genuine attempt to feel what another person is feeling, whereas sympathy can sometimes remain on the surface, merely acknowledging another person's distress without fully engaging with it. Think about the last time someone shared a problem with you. Did you feel simply sorry for them, or did you actively try to understand their experience from their perspective? The difference might seem subtle, but its impact on communication is profound.

Developing empathetic listening is like tuning your instrument finely before a big concert. It's all about getting the notes right to make beautiful music. In the realm of communication, this means actively engaging with the person speaking, not just nodding along while planning your next interruption. You can enhance your empathetic listening by really focusing on the speaker, observing their body language, and reflecting on their emotional state. Try to perceive the unsaid—tone, pace, and emotional undertones.

For instance, when someone talks about a stressful experience, their quickened speech or furrowed brows might give you clues about their emotional state. Reflecting on what you've heard can also be invaluable. Phrases like "It sounds like that was a really tough day for you" can show that you're not just hearing the words but also connecting with their feelings.

Expressing empathy in communication isn't just about understanding others and making your understanding evident. It's about letting others know you see and appreciate their perspective. This can be particularly effective in diverse situations where cultural, emotional, or situational differences might otherwise be a barrier. For example, if a team member from a different cultural background shares how they feel overlooked in group meetings, acknowledging their feelings and showing genuine interest in their views can make a significant difference. It tells them their feelings are valid and their contributions are valued. Techniques like mirroring the speaker's emotions or summarising their point of view can be very effective here. It shows that you are not just passively listening but actively engaging and valuing what they have to say.

In the tricky terrain of conflict resolution, empathy is your best guide. It helps shift the perspective from 'me against you' to 'us against the problem.' Empathy enables you to understand the motivations and emotions driving the other person's viewpoint, which can transform a contentious situation into a collaborative problem-solving session. It's about recognising the emotions at play and addressing them to find common ground. Suppose you're in a heated discussion with a colleague about the direction of a project. Acknowledging their concerns and expressing your understanding of their perspective will pave the way for a solution that respects both viewpoints. This doesn't mean you have to agree with everything they say. Still, by showing that you understand where they're coming from, you create an environment where solutions can be discussed openly and respectfully.

Empathy, therefore, is not just a passive emotional state but an active engagement tool that enhances communication. It allows for deeper human connections and can transform the way we interact with each other. Whether it's in a personal conversation or a professional meeting, empathy can lead to more productive and meaningful exchanges. It breaks down barriers and opens up channels of trust and understanding that are essential for effective communication. By embracing empathy, you become a better communicator and contribute to creating a more compassionate, understanding world.

1.5 CLARIFYING YOUR MESSAGE: THE KEY TO AVOIDING MISCOMMUNICATION

Have you ever played the game of telephone where one person whispers a message into the ear of another, and then it goes around the circle until the last person says it out loud? More often than not, the final message is hilariously garbled and bears little resemblance to the original. This isn't just a party trick; it starkly illustrates what can happen in our daily communications if clarity isn't prioritised. In both personal relationships and professional environments, the clarity of your message can be the difference between success and misunderstanding. It's not merely about what you say but ensuring the message is perceived as intended.

So, why is clear messaging crucial? Consider a scenario in a professional setting where you need to delegate tasks to your team. If your instructions are ambiguous, you might end up with incomplete projects or, worse, tasks done incorrectly. This can lead to frustration, wasted time, and resources. In personal contexts, unclear communication can lead to misunderstandings and conflicts, straining even the strongest relationships. Clear communication fosters better relationships, smoother workflows, and more effective problem-solving. It builds the foundation for trust and respect. When people understand what you expect or feel, they are more likely to align with your needs and expectations, reducing friction and increasing efficiency.

Now, let's move on to the strategies for enhancing clarity in your communication. It starts with knowing your message. Take a moment to distil exactly what you want to convey before you start speaking or writing. This focus prevents you from going off on tangents or clouding the main point. Structuring your message is also vital. Begin with a clear, concise statement of your main point and then elaborate as necessary. Use simple, direct language that matches the understanding of your audience. Avoid jargon unless you are certain the audience understands it. For instance, while discussing a project with your team, instead of saying, "We need to leverage our bandwidth to maximise synergies," you could say, "Let's collaborate efficiently to ensure everyone's workload is manageable, enhancing our team's output." This direct approach minimises the risk of misinterpretation.

Avoiding ambiguity is another crucial element. Ambiguity often creeps into communication when we use vague terms that can have multiple interpretations. Phrases like "as soon as possible" or "handle this issue" can mean different things to different people. Being specific eliminates ambiguity—tell your team to complete a task by a specific date or define the exact issue they need to address. Also, consider the power of visual aids. A chart, graph, or even a simple list can sometimes convey your points more clearly than verbal descriptions alone. For example, if you're explaining a complex workflow to your team, a flowchart can do wonders for their understanding compared to a verbal explanation alone.

Feedback loops are the last piece of the puzzle in achieving clear communication. They allow you to confirm that your message was understood as intended. After conveying your message, encourage questions and be open to clarifying doubts. Ask for feedback—try phrasing like, "Does that make sense to everyone?" or "What are your thoughts on this approach?" This ensures that your message is clear and fosters an interactive and inclusive communication environment. In personal settings, feedback can help you gauge whether your emotional message has been received. You might ask your partner, "How do you feel about what I just said?" to ensure your sentiments and not just the words are understood. This practice clarifies and deepens communication connections, making interactions more meaningful and effective.

In every aspect of your life, clarity in communication can dramatically enhance your interactions and outcomes. Whether it's giving instructions to your team, discussing plans with your partner, or negotiating a contract, taking the extra step to ensure your message is clear and understood as you intended can save you time and effort and safeguard your relationships and professional credibility. Remember, it's not just about being heard; it's about being understood. Clear communication is the bridge that connects intention with realisation, helping you navigate the complexities of human interactions in both your personal and professional life.

1.6 FEEDBACK DYNAMICS: GIVING AND RECEIVING WITH GRACE

Feedback, often dreaded and skirted around in corridors and coffee breaks, is one of our communication arsenal's most potent tools. Think of it not as a necessary evil but as a golden opportunity for growth and improvement. Both giving and receiving feedback requires finesse and under-standing, and when done well, they can transform average interactions into robust exchanges that foster growth, understanding, and productivity. Let's unwrap this package gently, shall we?

The Dual Role of Feedback

As a speaker, when you give feedback, you're essentially holding up a mirror to someone else's actions or behaviour, showing them how their performance aligns with expecta-tions or goals. It's a delicate task. Now flip the mirror around; as a listener receiving feedback, you're offered a window into how others perceive your actions. Both roles require empathy, precision, and care. For instance, in my early days at the financial firm, I remember giving feedback that I thought was direct and constructive, only to find it had discouraged rather than encouraged my team. It was a tough lesson in the power of words and delivery. I learned that feedback should be a balanced diet—nourishing yet palatable, designed to strengthen rather than weaken.

Constructive Feedback Techniques

Giving feedback that is constructive rather than critical is an art form. Begin with the mindset that your goal is to help, not to harm. It's not about pointing fingers but about pointing in the right direction. Always start from a place of observation rather than judgment. For example, instead of saying, "You failed to meet the project deadline," you might say, "I noticed the project was submitted past the deadline. Let's talk about what happened." This approach opens a dialogue rather than putting someone on the defensive. Be specific and focus on the behaviour, not the person. Use clear examples and avoid generalisations. Instead of saying, "Your work has been sloppy," specify with, "The last three reports have contained errors which could have been caught with a more thorough review." And remember, timing is crucial. Provide feedback as close to the event as possible, and do it in a setting conducive to a private and focused conversation.

Receiving Feedback Openly

Now, turning the tables to receiving feedback—it's not always easy to hear criticism, but it's crucial for our personal and professional development. Approach feedback with an open mind and a silent ego. When someone offers feedback, listen actively. This means not planning your rebuttal while the other person is speaking but really hearing their perspective. Ask clarifying questions if you're unsure about specific points, and resist the urge to defend yourself immediately. Reflect on the feedback given, and try to see it as valuable input for your growth path, not as a personal attack. I've found it helpful to keep a feedback journal where I note significant feedback and my reflections. This helps me track my progress and defuses some of the emotional charge that can come with receiving feedback.

Creating a Feedback Culture

Encouraging an environment where feedback is welcomed and valued starts at the top. If you're in a leadership role, model the feedback behaviours you want to see. Give regular, constructive feedback and receive it gracefully. Make it an integral part of your team's routine, maybe through regular review sessions or informal check-ins. Celebrate the successes and approach shortcomings as opportunities for growth. Creating a feedback-rich culture also means ensuring everyone feels safe expressing their thoughts and opinions. This psychological safety can transform a group of individuals into a cohesive, innovative team, where feedback is not feared but embraced as a pathway to excellence and mutual respect.

In wrapping up, remember that whether you're giving or receiving feedback, the goal is an improvement—of self, others, and the collective team. It's about building bridges, not burning them. It's about growing together, learning from each other, and moving forward with a shared purpose. Embrace feedback gracefully, and watch it transform your personal and professional life, one honest conversation at a time.

OVERCOMING COMMON COMMUNICATION BARRIERS

Imagine you're at a bustling networking event. The room is filled with potential connections, the air buzzing with opportunity. You spot someone you've been eager to meet who could be key to your next big career move. You stride over, extend a hand, and then... silence. Your mind goes blank, overshadowed by a nagging fear of saying something wrong. It's like your confidence took an untimely holiday, leaving you stranded. This chapter is your lifeline to communication confidence, helping you dismantle the barriers that keep you from expressing your best self.

2.1 BREAKING DOWN WALLS: OVERCOMING FEAR OF JUDGMENT

Understanding the Fear of Judgment

The fear of judgment can be paralyzing. It's the voice in your head that critiques every word you say and every move you make. But where does this voice come from? Often, it's a cocktail of past experiences, societal expectations, and personal insecurities. Maybe it's a harsh comment from a past boss that's lodged in your memory, or perhaps it's the pressure to live up to an ideal image portrayed in media. Understanding this fear is the first step in overcoming it. It's not about silencing that critical voice but learning to reduce its volume and challenge its validity. Recognize that everyone—yes, everyone—has moments of self-doubt. The key is not to let those moments dictate your actions. This understanding empowers you to take control of your communication, reducing the influence of fear and allowing you to express yourself more confidently.

Building Confidence

Confidence in communication doesn't always come naturally, but it's a skill that can be developed with practice and persistence. Start by acknowledging your strengths. Make a list if you have to. Are you a whiz with numbers? Do you have a knack for making people feel at ease? These are foundations upon which you can build your communication confidence. Next, set small, achievable goals for your interactions. Perhaps today, you'll make a point to speak up at least once during a meeting or compliment a colleague. Small wins can lead to significant gains in confidence. Also, consider the power of body language. Standing tall with your shoulders back and a smile can not only make you appear confident but actually make you feel more confident. It's like putting on a superhero cape. Suddenly, you're not just Clark Kent; you're Superman.

Safe Spaces for Communication

Creating environments where open communication is encouraged can significantly alleviate the fear of judgment. Whether at work or home, fostering a culture where people feel safe to express themselves without fear of ridicule or reprimand is crucial. In these spaces, every contribution is valued. Emphasize this value and actively listen when others speak. When people feel heard and valued, the fear of judgment diminishes, paving the way for more honest and productive communication. This emphasis on the value of every contribution makes everyone feel appreciated and respected, fostering a more open and inclusive communication environment.

Practical Exercises

Practical exercises can be incredibly effective in gradually overcoming the fear of being judged. One powerful technique is role-playing. It might feel awkward at first, but simulating various communication scenarios with a friend or mentor can prepare you for the real thing. Focus on scenarios that typically trigger your fear of judgment, and experiment with different responses. Another helpful exercise is video recording yourself. Record yourself delivering a speech or presentation, then watch it back. This can help you observe your communication style objectively and make adjustments as needed. It's also a great way to track your progress over time. Lastly, consider practicing mindfulness. Techniques like deep breathing or meditation can calm the mind and reduce the anxiety associated with fear of judgment. Before a potentially stressful communication situation, take a few minutes to centre yourself with some deep breaths. It's like hitting the reset button on your nervous system.

In this chapter, we've started to chip away at the daunting wall of communication barriers, focusing first on the pervasive fear of judgment. By understanding this fear, building your confidence, creating safe spaces, and practising through exercises, you're equipping yourself with the tools to not just cope but thrive in your communication efforts. Remember, every interaction is an opportunity to improve and grow, and every conversation is a step towards becoming a more confident communicator. As you continue to practice and apply these strategies, you'll find that the fear of judgment becomes less of an obstacle and more of a stepping stone on your path to effective communication.

2.2 NAVIGATING CULTURAL DIFFERENCES IN COMMUNICATION STYLES

In today's global village, the ability to communicate across cultural boundaries is not just a nice-to-have skill but a must-have. Picture this: you're on a video call with team members from four different countries, discussing the launch of a new product. Sounds straightforward, right? But here's the catch: each participant brings their cultural nuances to the table, influencing how they perceive information, express themselves, and make decisions. Recognizing and respecting these differences is crucial in ensuring that the conversation doesn't just generate more heat than light.

Recognizing Cultural Diversity

The first step in navigating this complex landscape is acknowledging that every culture has its unique set of communication styles. For instance, while a direct approach might be appreciated in the U.S., it could be perceived as rude in Japan, where indirectness is often valued. Similarly, while some cultures might value a rapid-fire exchange of ideas, others might prioritize thoughtful pauses and reflectiveness. For example, in a meeting with Japanese colleagues, you might notice that they often pause before responding. This is not a sign of indecision but a cultural norm that values thoughtful responses. Understanding these differences isn't just about reading up on cultural norms (though that certainly helps); it's about observing, listening, and being genuinely curious about how others communicate. It involves asking questions when you notice differences, not to challenge but to understand. This approach broadens your communication repertoire and shows respect for your colleagues' cultural backgrounds, paving the way for more effective and harmonious interactions.

Cultural Sensitivity

Developing sensitivity to these differences means more than just avoiding faux pas. It's about building a communication style that is both respectful and adaptable. For example, when you learn that maintaining eye contact is considered disrespectful in some cultures, you adapt by moderating your gaze during conversations with colleagues from those backgrounds. Or, when you understand that some cultures value a high-context communication style, where much is communicated through implicit messages and context rather than explicit words, you learn to read between the lines and offer more contextual information when communicating with individuals from those cultures. For instance, in a high-context culture, a simple 'yes' might mean 'I understand and will do it ', while in a low-context culture, the same response might mean 'I understand, but I'm not sure if I can do it '. Developing this sensitivity can feel like learning a new language—a language of cultural nuances and subtleties that can make or break your communication efforts.

Adapting Communication Strategies

Adapting your communication strategies in multicultural contexts often involves a delicate balancing act. You want to stay true to your own style to maintain authenticity, but you also need to stretch yourself to accommodate others' styles. This might mean toning down your usual exuberance in a culture that values restraint or stepping up your assertiveness in settings where directness is the norm. It's like being a chameleon, but one that changes its colours not just to blend in but to enrich the palette of the interaction. For example, suppose you are leading a team with members from both high-context and low-context cultures. In that case, you should provide clear, detailed instructions in written form to satisfy the needs of low-context individuals while also spending time in one-to-one conversations to address the high-context individuals' need for relational connection.

Bridging Cultural Gaps

Finally, effectively communicating across cultural boundaries often requires you to be a bridge-builder. This means not only adapting your communication style but also helping others to cross the cultural divide. It involves creating spaces where different styles are not just tolerated but valued. For instance, if you notice that some team members from quieter cultures are being overshadowed in meetings, you might institute a round-robin feedback system where everyone gets a chance to speak without interruption. Or, if you're working on a project with international stakeholders, you might set up a shared online platform where all communication is logged and clarified, ensuring that everyone, regardless of their communication style, is on the same page. These strategies do more than just smooth over cultural differences —they turn diversity into a dynamic engine of creativity and innovation, driving better outcomes for everyone involved.

Navigating cultural differences in communication is not just about avoiding misunderstandings but actively creating understanding. It's a skill that requires patience, empathy, and a willingness to learn and adapt. But the rewards are substantial: better relationships, more effective teamwork, and a richer, more diverse work environment. As the world becomes increasingly interconnected, your ability to communicate across cultures is not just an asset—it's essential. So, embrace the complexity, enjoy the learning, and watch your world and impact expand

2.3 THE ART OF ARTICULATION: EXPRESSING YOURSELF CLEARLY AND CONCISELY

Imagine you've landed an opportunity to present your project idea to senior management. The stakes are high, and the audience is demanding. You know your stuff, but the real challenge? It's about making them grasp your vision as clearly as you see it. This is where the art of articulation becomes your ally. Articulation isn't just about choosing the right words; it's about making your words create the right impact. When you articulate well, your message not only reaches the audience but also resonates with them, prompts action, and drives decisions.

Value of Articulation

Why fuss over articulation? Because in the realm of communication, clarity and conciseness are king and queen. Clear articulation means your audience spends less time deciphering your message and more time engaging with it. Consider the difference between a presentation laden with jargon and one that hits the sweet spot of simplicity and sophistication. Which one do you think holds the audience's attention? Effective articulation enhances understanding, ensures retention of the information, and can significantly influence the listener's response. It's like the difference between reading a dense legal document and a well-written novel. Both might have the same word count, but the novel likely keeps you hooked and emotionally invested because it's articulated in a way that's accessible and engaging.

Techniques for Better Articulation

So, how can you sharpen your articulation skills? It starts with the basics: enunciation and pace. Practice speaking clearly and at a pace that neither rushes the listeners nor bores them to tears. You can improve this through tongue twisters—yes, they're not just for kids! Try saying, "She sells sea shells by the sea shore" faster and faster without slurring. It's a fun and effective way to enhance your enunciation. Next, focus on tailoring your vocabulary to your audience. This doesn't mean dumbing down; it means making your message accessible. If you can replace a complex word with a simpler one without losing the essence, do it. For instance, use "help" instead of "facilitate" or "use" instead of "utilize." This small tweak can make your communication more relatable and less pretentious.

The Role of Preparation

Never underestimate the power of preparation. Knowing your material inside out is one thing, but thinking about how to present it clearly is another. Before any important communication, take a moment to outline your main points. What's the goal of your communication? What are the key takeaways for your audience? Structuring your thoughts in advance helps you stay on track and avoid going off on tangents. Use frameworks or outlines to prepare for a presentation or a meeting. This enables you to organize your thoughts and gives you a safety net to fall back on if you lose your train of thought.

Simplifying Complex Ideas

One of the hallmarks of great communicators is their ability to make complex ideas understandable. This skill is especially valuable in today's world, where we often must convey sophisticated information quickly and clearly. Start by breaking down complex ideas into smaller, digestible parts. Use analogies or metaphors to relate new ideas to familiar concepts. For example, if you're explaining blockchain technology, compare it to a ledger in a long-standing family business where transactions are recorded and visible to all family members, ensuring transparency and trust. Visual aids can also be a game-changer in simplifying complex ideas. A well-designed graph or chart can sometimes communicate what words cannot. Lastly, encourage feedback during your explanation. This not only helps you gauge understanding but also allows you to clarify points on the spot. By fostering interactive and responsive communication, you ensure that complex ideas are heard and understood.

As you continue to refine your articulation skills, remember that the goal is to bridge the gap between knowledge and communication. It's not just about what you know but how effectively you can share that knowledge with others. Whether in a boardroom, conference or casual conversation, your ability to express ideas clearly and concisely will set you apart. So take these strategies, practice diligently, and watch as your communication transforms from overlooked to outstanding.

2.4 MANAGING MISINTERPRETATIONS IN DIGITAL COMMUNICATION

In the digital age, our conversations often travel through screens, losing much of their human touch in the process. The lack of facial expressions, tone of voice, and body language can turn digital communication into a minefield of misunderstandings. Have you ever received an email that left you fuming, only to later discover that its tone was entirely misinterpreted? It's a common scenario in the realm of text-based communication, where intentions can be as murky as a foggy winter morning in Dublin. Here, the challenge isn't just about choosing the right words; it's about ensuring those words convey the intended meaning without the benefit of vocal tone or a reassuring smile.

One fundamental pitfall in digital communication is assuming that your message is as clear to your recipient as it is to you. When we communicate through digital channels, whether it's email, messaging apps, or social media, we lose the immediate feedback mechanisms inherent in face-to-face interactions. There's no nodding in agreement, no subtle shifts in posture to gauge understanding or confusion. This lack of feedback often leads to assumptions that everyone is on the same page, which isn't always true. To combat this, clarity becomes your best ally. Start by being concise; get to the point quickly without sacrificing politeness. Use simple, direct language that leaves little room for interpretation. For instance, instead of saying, "Could you get to this at some point?" specify, "Could you please complete this by end of day Tuesday?" This not only clarifies your expectations but also sets a tangible deadline.

Emojis, once confined to the casual chats of the digital world, have found their way into professional exchanges, helping clarify the tone that words on a screen can obscure. A well-placed smiley face can soften a request, convey friendliness, or lighten the mood. It's like adding a pinch of salt to a dish—it enhances the flavour without overwhelming it. However, the key is to use emojis judiciously. In professional settings, it's important to gauge the company culture and the preferences of the person you're communicating with. While your creative team colleague may appreciate a smiley face, it might not be suitable in a formal report to your stakeholders.

When misinterpretations occur—and they will—it's crucial to address them swiftly and with a focus on maintaining positive relationships. If you sense that your message may have been misunderstood, a quick follow-up can help clarify your intent. This could be as simple as sending another message providing more context or picking up the phone to clear up any confusion. When addressing a misunderstanding, approach the conversation with a resolution mindset, not blame. Use phrases like, "I wanted to clarify my earlier message to ensure we're on the same page," rather than, "You misunderstood my previous email." This non-confrontational approach fosters a more open and constructive dialogue.

Navigating the nuances of digital communication requires a blend of clarity, empathy, and adaptability. By being mindful of the challenges, employing strategies for clear communication, and using digital tools effectively, you can minimize misunderstandings and maintain robust, positive interactions, even across the digital divide. Remember, every email; every message is a thread in the fabric of your relationships; making each one count helps weave stronger connections.

2.5 FROM ANXIETY TO AUTHORITY: TRANSFORMING NERVOUS ENERGY

Understanding Communication Anxiety

Let's tackle a common ghost that haunts many of us before a big presentation or during a crucial conversation—communication anxiety. It's that flutter in your stomach, the sweaty palms, the racing heart just before you step up to speak. Fundamentally, it's your body's flight-or-fight response kicking in, not because you're facing a real threat but because your brain perceives social judgment or rejection as a danger. This response is rooted deeply in our evolutionary need to belong to a group for survival. So, when you're about to speak in front of an audience, your brain might interpret their attention as scrutiny, triggering anxiety. Understandably, this can feel overwhelming, but recognising this physiological and psychological basis of speaking anxiety is pivotal. It empowers you to acknowledge that your feelings are a natural response, not a sign of incompetence or weakness. This understanding is the first step in transforming nervous energy from a paralyzing force into a propelling one.

Transforming Anxiety into Confidence

Now, let's shift gears from why you're anxious to how you can use that anxiety to your advantage. Transforming anxiety into confidence might sound like a bit of magic, and in some ways, it is— it's about channelling the same energy that fuels your nerves into fueling your performance. Start by reframing your perspective. Instead of viewing public speaking as a threat, try to see it as an opportunity to share your knowledge, tell your story, or persuade your audience about something you care about. This shift in mindset can reduce the intensity of your anxiety. Another technique is to use your nervous energy as a rehearsal catalyst. Use the adrenaline rush to energise your preparation process. Practice your speech or presentation multiple times until you feel more in control. Each run-through builds muscle memory, and the familiarity of what you're about to do can significantly dampen anxiety. Additionally, before you take the stage or enter the meeting room, perform some quick physical exercises like stretching or pacing. This can help burn off some of that excess adrenaline and lessen the physical symptoms of anxiety.

Practicing Mindfulness

Mindfulness is like a secret garden that offers refuge from the bustling city of your anxious thoughts. It's about being present in the moment, aware of your thoughts and feelings without judgment. Integrating mindfulness into your communication practices can help manage anxiety by grounding your thoughts when they start spiralling into the territory of 'what ifs.' Start with simple breathing exercises. Focus on your breath, inhale slowly for a count of four, hold for a count of four, and exhale for a count of four. This controlled breathing helps regulate your nervous system and brings your focus back to the present. Another mindfulness technique is visualisation. Before a speaking event, take a moment to close your eyes and visualise yourself successfully delivering your speech. See the audience engaging with your content, and hear yourself speaking clearly and confidently. This mental rehearsal primes your brain to perform as visualised, often reducing anxiety as you align with the successful outcome you've already 'experienced.'

Building a Personal Empowerment Plan

Creating a personal empowerment plan is like drawing a map that leads you from anxiety to authority in communication. This plan should be tailored to recognise your unique triggers and strengths. Begin by setting specific, achievable goals for your communication endeavours. Perhaps you aim to speak up at least once in every meeting, or maybe you want to lead a workshop by the end of the quarter. Whatever your goals, write them down. Break them into smaller, manageable tasks and set deadlines for each. For each task, identify the skills or knowledge you need to succeed and how you can acquire them. Do you need to improve your slide-making skills? Or perhaps a storytelling workshop could enhance your presentations. Include these learning goals in your plan. Regular reflection is also a vital part of your empowerment plan. After each speaking engagement, take some time to reflect on what went well and what could be improved. Celebrate your successes, no matter how small, and use setbacks as learning opportunities. This continuous cycle of setting goals, learning, performing, and reflecting creates a positive feedback loop that gradually builds your confidence and competence in communication.

By understanding the roots of communication anxiety, leveraging techniques to transform this anxiety, practising mindfulness, and building a structured empowerment plan, you equip yourself not only to manage but also to capitalize on the energy that nervousness brings. Each step forward in this plan is a step away from anxiety and towards becoming a more confident and authoritative communicator.

2.6 SILENCE ISN'T ALWAYS GOLDEN: THE DANGERS OF WITHHOLDING COMMUNICATION

The adage "Silence is golden" might hold true in certain scenarios, like during a poignant movie scene or when soaking in the serene quiet of dawn. However, in personal and professional communication, holding back your thoughts more often leads to murky waters than tranquillity. Consider the times when unspoken grievances or unshared ideas have snowballed into misunderstandings or conflicts. In these instances, silence isn't just a void of words; it's a breeding ground for confusion and resentment. This withholding of communication, whether due to fear, indifference, or misunderstanding, can severely undermine relationships and team dynamics.

Risks of Withholding

The peril of withheld communication is that it allows narratives to be written without input from all parties. When you don't voice your thoughts or feelings, you leave room for others to interpret your silence according to their biases or fears. For example, if a team leader doesn't communicate the rationale behind a decision, team members might assume it was made with bias or without a full understanding of the situation. This can lead to feelings of distrust and alienation. In personal relationships, not expressing your feelings or concerns can lead to a buildup of resentment, which might erupt over something trivial, surprising even those who thought everything was fine. The key takeaway? Unspoken words can sometimes speak louder than spoken ones, often saying all the wrong things.

Encouraging Open Dialogue

Creating an environment that promotes open dialogue involves nurturing a culture of valuing sharing over silence. This can be fostered by setting explicit expectations for communication within your team or family. Regular meetings where everyone is encouraged and expected to speak up or dedicated 'listening sessions' can be institutionalized. These platforms should be seen not just as formalities but as vital valves for releasing pressure and garnering diverse perspectives. In these settings, acknowledge and validate the contributions of all speakers to reinforce the value of open dialogue. Remember, the goal is to make sharing thoughts as natural as breathing—essential and effortless.

Overcoming the Fear of Speaking Up

The trepidation about voicing thoughts can be paralyzing. To ease this, start by recognizing that this fear stems from how others might perceive your words. Counter this by building a supportive communication environment. One practical approach is the 'yes, and...' exercise borrowed from improvisational theatre. In this exercise, every idea a team member contributes is met with "yes, and..." rather than "but..." or silence. This validates the initial idea and encourages a constructive buildup of the original thought. Furthermore, enhance your personal comfort with speaking up by starting in smaller, less intimidating groups before addressing larger audiences. Gradually, as your comfort grows, so will your confidence.

The Power of Vulnerable Communication

Embracing vulnerability in communication is about showing that it's okay to share not just successes and certainties but also doubts and failures. Vulnerable communication fosters deeper connections, as it invites others to engage with the real you, not just the always-composed facade. This doesn't mean sharing every insecurity at every turn; rather, it's about being honest in your interactions. For instance, a leader admitting they don't have all the answers but are committed to finding solutions can inspire teams to contribute more openly and fearlessly. Vulnerability can be particularly powerful in building trust, as it signifies that you value authenticity over perfection.

This exploration of the pitfalls of withheld communication and the strategies to encourage openness and vulnerability sets the stage for better interactions and richer, more meaningful relationships. Each step toward open dialogue and vulnerable sharing is a step away from the shadows of misunderstanding and conflict, guiding us towards a clearer, more connected way of interacting.

As we wrap up this chapter, remember that communication is not just about exchanging information but also about sharing ourselves—our thoughts, fears, and hopes. We enrich our interactions and deepen our connections by fostering open, honest dialogue, encouraging everyone to voice their thoughts, and embracing vulnerability. These practices are not just antidotes to the risks of silence; they are the building blocks of robust personal and professional relationships.

As we move forward, let these insights guide you not just in overcoming communication barriers but in transforming your interactions into gateways for genuine connection and understanding. Ready to turn the page? Let's continue to unravel the complexities of effective communication together.

BUILDING STRONGER PERSONAL RELATIONSHIPS THROUGH COMMUNICATION

When it comes to personal relationships, communication isn't just a tool; it's the water that nourishes your relationships' garden. Whether it's with your partner, a close friend, or even a colleague you've grown fond of, how you communicate can mean the difference between a blossoming garden and a neglected patch of weeds. In this chapter, we're going to roll up our sleeves and get our hands dirty in the garden of love and personal connections, starting with how to cultivate romantic relationships through masterful communication.

3.1 SPEAKING THE LANGUAGE OF LOVE: COMMUNICATION IN ROMANTIC RELATIONSHIPS

Understanding Love Languages

Have you ever given a thoughtful gift only to find it didn't excite your partner as much as you hoped? Or perhaps you've cleaned the entire house expecting a thrilled response, only to receive a casual "thanks"? Before doubting your partner's gratitude or gift-picking skills, consider this: you might be speaking different love languages. Dr Gary Chapman's concept of the Five Love Languages suggests that everyone has a preferred way of receiving love: Words of Affirmation, Acts of Service, Receiving Gifts, Quality Time, and Physical Touch. Understanding and speaking your partner's love language can transform your relationship. It's like having a direct line to their heart. Suddenly, you're no longer just saying "I love you"; you're showing it in a way they understand and appreciate deeply. Start by observing what makes your partner feel most loved, or ask them directly. Then, make an effort to express your love in that language consistently. It's like learning to say "I love you" in French to charm a Parisian lover—it's more work, but oh la la, the results are worth it!

Conflict Resolution

Now, let's talk about the inevitable: conflicts. They're not a sign of a weak relationship but a natural part of sharing your life with someone. The key to conflict resolution lies not in avoidance but in tackling it healthily. Start by acknowledging that both parties have legitimate viewpoints. Approach conflicts with a problem-solving attitude rather than a combative one. Use "I" statements to express how you feel instead of "you" statements, which can sound accusatory, like "I feel upset when we leave decisions to the last minute" instead of "You always mess up our plans." Also, really listen to understand, not to counter-attack. Sometimes, conflicts escalate simply because one or both parties don't feel heard. Take turns speaking and listening. Remember, it's not about winning an argument; it's about understanding each other and finding a solution that respects both perspectives. Think of it as a dance, not a battle—sometimes you lead, sometimes you follow, but the goal is always to stay in rhythm together.

Communicating Needs and Desires

Being open about your needs and desires can be scary, making you vulnerable. But it's also one of the most potent ways to deepen intimacy. Clear communication about what you need and desire abolishes guesswork and disappointment. It sets a clear path for your partner to love you in the way you want to be loved. Start small if this feels daunting. Share something you've been hesitant to say, perhaps about a hobby you want to pursue together or a habit of theirs that bothers you. Be kind but honest, and create a safe space for them to do the same. This mutual sharing fosters a deep sense of intimacy and trust, reinforcing the idea that your relationship is a safe harbour for your truths.

Listening with the Heart

Empathetic listening is about tuning in with your heart, not just your ears. It's about hearing the words and feeling the emotions behind them. When your partner speaks, especially about something laden with emotion, try to feel what they are experiencing. For instance, if your partner is excited about a new opportunity, try to share in their excitement. Reflect back what you understand, both in words and emotions, like 'It sounds like you're really excited about this opportunity, and I can see why it means so much to you.' This kind of listening validates their feelings and shows that you're not just a bystander in their experiences; you're right there with them. It's a way of saying, 'I'm with you, no matter what,' without actually using words. This deep, empathetic connection is the glue that holds relationships together through thick and thin.

Navigating the seas of romantic relationships isn't always smooth sailing, but with the right communication tools, it's easier to weather the storms and enjoy the sunny days together. By understanding and applying the principles of love languages, conflict resolution, open sharing of needs and desires, and empathetic listening, you're equipped to build a relationship that's not just about surviving but thriving. Remember, good communication is not the icing on the cake of a relationship; it's the main ingredient. So, keep these tools handy and watch your relationship transform into a more loving, understanding, and fulfilling partnership.

3.2 FAMILY DYNAMICS: IMPROVING COMMUNICATION AT HOME

When it comes to family, each member can sometimes feel like they're speaking a different language, even if you all grew up under the same roof. Understanding and adapting to these unique communication styles can feel a bit like being a translator, ensuring everyone not only speaks but also understands and respects each other's linguistic quirks. Let's start by recognizing that each family member may have a distinct way of expressing themselves. For instance, one child might be very verbal, sharing every detail of their day, while another might prefer showing you their day's highlights through actions or drawings. As the 'family linguist,' it's your role to tune into these different styles. This might mean asking direct, open-ended questions to the talkative child while spending more quiet time engaged in activities with the less verbal one, giving them space to open up in their comfort zone. It's about making sure everyone feels heard and understood on their terms.

Creating a safe space for expression in a family setting goes beyond just being physically present. It's about building an environment where each member feels emotionally secure enough to share their thoughts and feelings, no matter how trivial or profound. This can be established by regular family meetings where everyone, regardless of age, gets a turn to voice their opinions and feelings without interruption. During these sessions, reinforce the idea that every emotion is valid and that it's okay to express feelings without fear of judgment or immediate solutions. Sometimes, just being heard is all someone needs. To maintain this safe space, consistently reinforce that home is not just a place but a feeling of being supported and understood, a haven where each family member can truly be themselves.

Setting boundaries within a family is crucial and should be done with compassion and clarity. Boundaries help define where one person's comfort zone ends and another's begins, fostering mutual respect and understanding. When setting these limits, especially with children, it's helpful to explain why they're necessary, linking them to values like respect, privacy, or safety. For example, you might set a boundary around personal space, explaining that just like they have their own room where they can feel comfortable, you need certain spaces or times to be respected for your activities. When these boundaries are crossed, address the issue with understanding rather than frustration. Explain how the breach affects you or others in the family, emphasizing the importance of respecting each other's space and needs as a way of showing love and respect.

While challenging, dealing with conflicts within the family is essential for maintaining a healthy dynamic. Start by acknowledging that conflict is a normal part of relationships, not a failure of family harmony. Approach conflicts with a problem-solving mentality, focusing on the issue at hand rather than personal attacks. For instance, if siblings are fighting over shared resources like the television or computer, help them see the larger picture of fairness and sharing, guiding them to a discussion about scheduling and mutual respect. Teach them negotiation skills, like offering something in return rather than just demanding what they want. In more intense conflicts, especially between adults, take time to cool down before addressing the issue to avoid saying things in the heat of the moment that may be regretted later. When resolving these issues, aim for solutions that acknowledge everyone's feelings and needs, reinforcing the idea that the family works best when everyone feels valued and involved.

Navigating the complex world of family communication requires patience, empathy, and a bit of creativity. You strengthen the fabric of your family by recognizing and respecting individual communication styles, fostering a safe environment for open dialogue, setting compassionate boundaries, and managing conflicts constructively. Each conversation, each shared moment, builds the foundation for a family that isn't just connected by blood or law but bonded by understanding, respect, and love. As you continue to apply these principles, watch how they not only improve communication but also deepen the connections within your family, making every interaction more meaningful and every conflict less daunting.

3.3 FRIENDSHIP AND SOCIAL CONNECTIONS: KEEPING THE LINES OPEN

In the tapestry of our lives, friendships are the vibrant threads that add colour and warmth. But as with any valuable relationship, maintaining the richness of these threads over time requires care, attention, and, of course, skillful communication. Have you ever considered how friendships evolve or, perhaps, why some fizz out? Much like plants need water to thrive, friendships need the nourishment of consistent and meaningful interactions. Let's consider how you can keep these bonds strong and vibrant, even as life whirls around with its myriad distractions.

Maintaining Long-Term Friendships

The secret sauce to sustaining long-term friendships lies in the commitment to stay connected and the quality of your interactions. As we age, our lives can diverge paths—careers, families, and personal pursuits can make scheduling a coffee date feel like coordinating a space launch. However, the effort to stay in touch, whether it's a quick text to share a memory or a call to celebrate a milestone, sends a clear message: you matter to me. Prioritising face-to-face meetings whenever possible is irreplaceable for creating shared memories and deepening bonds. For friends who live miles apart, technology offers a lifeline. A video call can bridge the physical gap, allowing you to share life updates or enjoy a 'virtual' coffee together. And remember, it's not about the frequency of communication but its quality. Even if you connect less often, ensuring the interactions are heartfelt and genuine can keep the friendship thriving.

Digital Communication with Friends

In an era where a 'like' or a 'share' can substitute for a conversation, balancing digital interactions with face-to-face communication becomes crucial. Digital tools are fantastic for keeping the lines open, especially with those far away. They allow for spontaneous' thinking of you' messages or sharing a meme that sparks laughter. However, these should complement, not replace, the richer, more nuanced interactions that face-to-face or voice-to-voice communications provide. Use digital platforms to set up in-person gatherings or to continue conversations from where you left off during your last meetup. Be mindful of how you use these tools—passive scrolling through a friend's social media is not communication. Engage actively. Comment with thought, send messages that add value, and use these platforms to enhance, not overshadow your real-world interactions.

Navigating Difficult Conversations with Friends

Even the strongest friendships can face turbulence. Addressing sensitive topics with care and respect can prevent a rift, whether it's a misunderstanding or a more serious disagreement. Start these conversations with an open mind and a calm demeanour. It's essential to approach from a place of wanting to understand rather than wanting to be right. Frame your concerns with sensitivity, using "I feel" statements to express your feelings without blaming. For instance, saying, "I felt hurt when you didn't support my decision" is more constructive than saying, "You never support me." Be prepared to listen to their side of the story—communication is a two-way street, after all. When handled thoughtfully, these conversations can deepen trust and understanding within the friendship, showing that it can withstand even the tough moments.

Active Support and Empathy

Being a supportive friend isn't just about cheering from the sidelines; it's about stepping into the arena with them when needed. This means actively listening to their concerns, cele-brating their successes as if they were your own, and providing comfort during tough times. Show empathy by validating their feelings—let them know it's okay to feel the way they do. Sometimes, all a friend needs is to feel understood. Other times, they may need advice or practical help. Gauge the situation and ask how you can best support them. Perhaps it's helping them prepare for a job interview, offering a ride to an appointment, or simply providing a listening ear. By being genuinely engaged and responsive to their needs, you strengthen the emotional connection, reinforcing that your friendship is a safe and supportive haven.

In navigating the complexities of maintaining and nurturing friendships, remember that communication is the bridge that connects your shared past with the present and future. It's about being present, genuine, and showing up—whether in person, through a screen, or over a call. As we move forward, consider how each interaction can build or maintain the bridge between you and your friends. With each word and gesture, you have the power to strengthen these vital connections, ensuring they continue to enrich your life and withstand the tests of time and distance.

3.4 HANDLING PERSONAL CONFLICTS WITH FINESSE

When it comes to personal conflicts, it often feels like navigating a minefield blindfolded. One wrong step, and you're in the middle of an emotional explosion. However, understanding the root causes of these conflicts can turn that blindfold into a clear set of goggles, helping you to tread carefully and effectively. Often, conflicts don't just arise from the immediate issues at hand but stem from underlying frustrations, unmet expectations, or miscommunications that have piled up over time. It's like ignoring a leaking pipe because it's just a few drops, only to come home to a flooded kitchen one day. To get to the heart of the conflict, start by peeling back the layers of the immediate problem to explore what's been brewing underneath. This might involve asking probing questions that go beyond the surface or reflecting on past interactions that might have contributed to the buildup. For instance, if you find yourself repeatedly arguing over seemingly minor issues like household chores, it might signify deeper feelings of unfairness or taken-for-granted efforts that need to be addressed. By identifying these root causes, you can address the real issues, preventing them from resurfacing and turning every small disagreement into a potential battlefield.

Finding common ground is like discovering a bridge over a chasm—it allows both parties to meet halfway, ensuring that everyone's needs are considered without anyone feeling like they've lost a part of themselves in the process. This art of compromise is essential in resolving conflicts in a way that strengthens relationships rather than weakening them. Start by acknowledging each other's viewpoints as valid, even if you disagree with them. This recognition can soften the ground for discussion, making it easier to find areas of agreement. Then, explore different options together, looking for solutions that might satisfy each person's most important needs. Sometimes, this might mean alternating between preferences; for example, choosing one person's preference for holiday destinations this year and the other's next year. Other times, it might involve blending elements from each person's desires to create a new plan that excites everyone involved. The key is to approach these negotiations with flexibility, creativity, and a genuine desire for mutual satisfaction, not a win-lose outcome.

Expressing disagreement constructively is an art form that can turn potentially relationship-damaging situations into opportunities for growth and understanding. It starts with the realisation that disagreement is a natural part of any relationship. The goal isn't to avoid disagreement but to learn how to express it in ways that are respectful and constructive. Use "I" statements to express your feelings about the situation rather than blaming or pointing fingers. For example, say, "I feel overwhelmed when we leave planning our finances to the last minute," instead of "You never care about our budget!" This approach focuses on your feelings and experiences rather than assigning fault. Also, listen actively to the other person's point of view. This doesn't just mean hearing their words but really trying to understand where they're coming from. Validate their feelings, even if you see things differently. For instance, you might say, "I see why you felt upset about that; it wasn't my intention to make you feel overlooked." This kind of empathetic engagement can diffuse tension and open up space for more constructive problem-solving.

Rebuilding trust and communication after a conflict is crucial. It's about fixing the emotional pipes and ensuring the pressure doesn't build up again. Start by openly discussing what went wrong and why. This conversation can be tough, but it's essential for clearing the air and setting the stage for rebuilding. Apologize where apologies are due, and be specific about what you're sorry for. This shows that you're taking responsibility for your part in the conflict.

Then, discuss ways to prevent similar issues in the future. This might involve setting new communication rules or adjusting some of the expectations that contributed to the conflict.

Most importantly, give it time. Rebuilding trust doesn't happen overnight. It requires consistent effort and patience from both sides. Keep the lines of communication open, continue to share your thoughts and feelings, and slowly but surely, you'll see the trust return stronger for the challenges it has overcome.

3.5 EMPATHY IN ACTION: DEEPENING PERSONAL BONDS

Empathy, often tossed around in discussions about personal and professional relationships, is more than just a buzzword —it's the glue that can hold relationships together, allowing for a deeper connection and understanding between individuals. When we talk about empathetic listening, we're not just referring to nodding along while someone talks; it's about truly engaging with and feeling the emotions they are expressing. Imagine you're listening to a friend who's going through a tough time. Instead of just waiting for them to finish so you can offer advice or share your own story, you immerse yourself in their experience, you feel their sadness, their frustration, or their joy. This level of understanding requires you to fully concentrate on the speaker, avoiding distractions like glancing at your phone or thinking about your next appointment. One practical tip is to mirror the emotions you perceive in their voice and facial expressions. If they're sharing something sad, it's okay to show sadness on your face, too, which communicates that you are with them in their feelings, not just as a bystander but as someone who truly cares. Additionally, paraphrasing what you've heard and gently asking clarifying questions can enhance your understanding and show that you are genuinely engaged. This doesn't just make the other person feel valued; it often leads to deeper conversations that strengthen the bonds of your relationship.

Empathy plays a crucial role in providing emotional support because it goes beyond superficial responses to someone's issues. It involves recognising the emotions behind the words and responding in a way that addresses them. For instance, if someone feels overwhelmed with work, instead of offering the generic "Just hang in there," which might come off as dismissive, you could say, "It sounds like you're under a lot of pressure. What's the most challenging part for you right now?" This kind of response not only acknowledges their feelings but also opens the door for them to share more about their experience, which itself can be relieving. Being empathetic in your communication makes people feel heard and seen, which can be incredibly comforting and reassuring. It transforms simple conversations into moments of connection and healing, reinforcing the support system that relationships are meant to provide.

Applying empathy in diverse relationships—with colleagues, friends from different cultures, or acquaintances—can sometimes be challenging due to differing perspectives and experiences. However, the core of empathy is the same across all relationships: the attempt to understand another's feelings and viewpoint from their frame of reference. It means stepping into their shoes, regardless of where they stand. This might require you to sometimes set aside your own biases or preconceptions, which isn't always easy. For example, if you have a colleague from a culture where direct criticism is considered rude, understanding their indirect way of giving feedback is crucial. It's about respecting and validating their communication style, even if it's not your own. This doesn't mean you have to agree with everyone's viewpoints or emotions, but acknowledging their right to feel a certain way can help bridge gaps in understanding and foster a more inclusive environment.

One of the biggest challenges to empathy is overcoming personal biases—those preconceived notions and judgments we all carry, often without realising it. These biases can cloud our ability to see things from another person's perspective. The first step to overcoming these is awareness —recognising that you have biases and actively working to identify them. Reflect on your interactions and ask yourself if certain patterns keep emerging. Do you find it harder to empathise with certain types of people or viewpoints? Why might that be? Engaging with diverse groups and exposing yourself to different perspectives can also help dismantle these biases. It's a process, and it doesn't change overnight, but every step towards understanding and empathy is a step towards richer, more connected relationships. As you practice empathy, both in listening and in supporting others, you'll find it transforms your relationships and enriches your personal growth, making you a more understanding, compassionate person.

3.6 THE POWER OF VULNERABILITY IN PERSONAL DISCOURSE

Vulnerability often gets a bad rap as something akin to a chink in your armour, a sign of weakness that others can exploit. But let's flip that narrative on its head and consider vulnerability in a new light—as a profound strength that enhances genuine communication and deepens connections. When you allow yourself to be vulnerable, you're not just sharing your triumphs or a polished version of your life; you're also sharing the struggles and the not-so-glamorous bits. This kind of transparency can act like a bridge, showing others that it's okay to be human and not always have it all together. Think of vulnerability as the secret ingredient that can transform superficial interactions into meaningful exchanges. It's about letting your guard down and showing your true self, which in turn invites others to do the same.

Sharing personal stories is one of the most powerful ways to harness this strength. You open the door to a more authentic relationship when you share your experiences, especially those that might show you in a less-than-perfect light. For instance, sharing a mistake you made at work or a personal challenge you're struggling with can be incredibly freeing. It not only lightens your emotional load but also sets the stage for others to share their own stories. This kind of exchange can rapidly build trust and foster a sense of camaraderie and support. Remember, it's not about airing your dirty laundry for the sake of drama; it's about choosing to share personal insights that are relevant and can lead to mutual understanding and support.

However, opening up can be daunting. The fear of being vulnerable—of being judged or rejected—can be paralyzing. But there are ways to ease into this vulnerability without feeling like you're jumping off a cliff. Start small. You don't have to share your deepest secrets right off the bat. Begin by sharing small truths or feelings in situations where you feel relatively safe. Pay attention to how others respond.

In most cases, you'll find that your openness is met with warmth and openness in return. Gradually, as your comfort level increases, so can the depth of your disclosures. Another effective strategy is to practice self-compassion. Be as kind to yourself as you would be to a friend. Recognizing that everyone has vulnerabilities can make sharing yours feel less daunting.

Balancing vulnerability with boundaries is crucial. It's about knowing how much to share, with whom, and when. Not every setting or every person will be right for sharing personal stories or feelings. It's okay to choose to be more open with certain people or in certain situations. Setting these boundaries doesn't diminish your vulnerability; rather, it ensures that you're opening up in ways that are respectful to your own emotional needs and conducive to building healthy relationships. For instance, being vulnerable in a close friendship can strengthen that bond, but the same level of openness might not be appropriate or beneficial in a professional setting.

Navigating the realm of personal discourse with vulnerability is not without its challenges, but the rewards—deeper connections, enhanced trust, and greater authenticity—are well worth the effort. By reframing vulnerability as a strength, sharing personal stories, easing the fears associated with openness, and setting healthy boundaries, you can transform your interactions from superficial exchanges to rich, meaningful dialogues. This approach not only enriches your personal relationships but also brings a greater sense of authenticity and fulfilment to your life.

As we wrap up this exploration of vulnerability in communication, remember that the courage to be vulnerable is not about weakness but about embracing the full spectrum of human experience—ups, downs, and everything in between. It's about showing up as your true self, which in turn allows others to do the same. This chapter has equipped you to navigate vulnerability confidently and set the groundwork for deeper, more authentic connections. As you move forward, carry these insights with you as tools and companions on your journey to more meaningful interactions and relationships.

MASTERING SOCIAL INTERACTIONS

Navigating the bustling maze of social interactions can sometimes feel like being a contestant on a game show where you're constantly guessing the next right move. Whether it's a quick chat by the coffee machine or a casual dinner with new neighbours, the art of small talk and casual conversations often sets the stage for deeper connections. Let's roll up our sleeves and dive into the nuances of mastering these everyday interactions with finesse and a bit of charm, ensuring you leave a memorable impression that paves the way for meaningful relationships.

4.1 SMALL TALK, BIG IMPACT: MASTERING CASUAL CONVERSATIONS

The Purpose of Small Talk: Understanding small talk's role in building rapport and trust

Think of small talk not as trivial chit-chat but as the delicate stitching that binds the fabric of social interactions. It's the initial threads we weave to connect with new acquaintances or to maintain bonds with those we sporadically see. But why is small talk so important? It serves as a low-risk evaluation phase where people gauge each other's personalities and find common ground. These light conversations are crucial in a world where trust can be as elusive as a perfectly cooked steak. They allow us to establish a comfort zone with others, showing that we're friendly and approachable without diving into potentially contentious topics. For instance, discussing the weather or a popular TV show might seem superficial, but it's a way of saying, "I'm here, I'm friendly, and I'm open to engaging with you." This can be particularly impactful in professional settings, where building trust can lead to collaborations and opportunities down the line.

Topics for Engaging Small Talk: Ideas for light, engaging topics suitable for various social settings

Choosing the right topics for small talk is a bit like selecting the right appetizer for a meal—it should whet the appetite for a potential friendship but not overwhelm it with too much spice right away. Stick to universally relatable—and positive—topics like travel, food, movies, or books, which are generally safe and can pique interest. For instance, asking someone if they've seen the latest blockbuster or tried a new restaurant in town can open up a dialogue that might reveal shared interests. Avoid polarizing topics like politics or religion, which can quickly turn a pleasant exchange into a heated debate. Remember, small talk aims to lay a smooth runway for a potential deeper conversation, not to dive into the deep end immediately.

Transitioning Beyond Small Talk: Tips for smoothly moving from casual to more meaningful conversations

While small talk is a great starting point, the magic of social interactions often lies in those deeper, more meaningful conversations that follow. Transitioning there smoothly requires skill and timing. Pay close attention to cues that the person is interested in delving deeper. This could be them asking you more personal questions or them elaborating extensively on a topic. To facilitate this transition, you might share a slightly more personal experience related to the topic at hand, which invites reciprocity. For example, if the conversation starts with a discussion about movies, you could share an anecdote about how a particular film influenced your perspective on a subject. This subtly shifts the gear from surface-level chat to more substantial dialogue, paving the way for a genuine connection.

Practising Mindful Listening in Small Talk: The importance of showing genuine interest and attention

Mindful listening is an essential ingredient in the recipe for successful social interactions. It's about being fully present in the conversation, not just waiting for your turn to speak but actively listening and responding to what the other person is saying. This shows that you value their thoughts and are engaged in the interaction, which can make all the difference in how they perceive you. To practice mindful listening, focus on maintaining eye contact, nodding in acknowledgement, and avoiding interruptions. Reflect back what they say occasionally to show you're keeping up, and ask relevant questions that deepen the dialogue. This level of attentiveness not only makes the other person feel respected and heard but also significantly enhances the quality of the interaction, making even a brief chat a memorable one.

In mastering the art of casual conversations, you equip yourself with the tools not just to start relationships but to potentially deepen them. Each interaction, no matter how brief, is a stepping stone to building networks of trust and friendship. So next time you find yourself in a scenario that calls for small talk, embrace it with enthusiasm and a dash of strategy. And remember, knowing how to gracefully exit a conversation is just as important as starting one. If you sense the conversation is winding down, you can say something like, 'It was great talking to you. I'll let you get back to [what they were doing].' This shows respect for their time and leaves a positive impression. Who knows? That chat about the weather might just be the beginning of a beautiful friendship.

4.2 READING THE ROOM: ADAPTING YOUR COMMUNICATION STYLE

Imagine walking into a room buzzing with chatter, some clusters of people laughing, a few deep in serious discussion. Each social setting is a unique tapestry of dynamics, and your ability to read these cues is like having a roadmap. Understanding the underlying social dynamics can make or break your interactions, whether it's a high-energy startup party or a formal corporate dinner. It begins with a quick scan of the room—observe who's talking to whom, the body language being exhibited, and the overall energy of the space. Are people leaning in, animated with hands flying about, or are they more reserved, with conversations taking a quieter tone? This initial assessment helps you gauge the mood and adjust your approach accordingly. For example, in a lively setting, you might join in with light-hearted banter or share an amusing anecdote to blend in with the energy of the room. Conversely, in a more subdued or formal gathering, adopting a measured, thoughtful way of speaking can help in matching the tone of the environment.

As you navigate through these social waters, adapting your communication style becomes crucial. Think of it as adjusting the sails of your boat depending on the wind's direction. You'll want to trim down any rambling stories if you find yourself in a group that values concise, straight-to-the-point dialogue. On the other hand, if the group enjoys detailed storytelling, feel free to elaborate a bit more, giving colour and context to your narratives. The key here is flexibility—being able to switch gears without losing your authentic voice. It's not about being a chameleon who changes colours at will but more about adjusting the shade of your natural colour to fit the picture. Also, pay attention to how others are reacting to your communication. Are they engaged and nodding along, or do they seem distracted? This feedback is invaluable, allowing you to continuously refine your approach in real time.

Cultural sensitivity is another critical piece of the puzzle, especially in our globalized world, where social functions are melting pots of diverse cultures. Each culture has its own set of communication norms and etiquette. For instance, in some cultures, maintaining eye contact is seen as a sign of respect and honesty; in others, it might be perceived as confrontational. Similarly, the concept of personal space varies widely—what's considered a respectful distance in one culture might be seen as standoffish in another. Educating yourself about these differences can prevent potential faux pas and show respect for others' cultural backgrounds. It's about embracing diversity not just as a concept but as a practical aspect of everyday interactions. Whether it's knowing when to shake hands or bow or understanding the appropriate topics of conversation, being culturally adept enriches your social engagements. It showcases your respect for the varied tapestry of human backgrounds.

Finally, let's talk about the role of non-verbal cues. These often speak louder than words. Your posture, gestures, and facial expressions can communicate confidence, openness, or discomfort, often without a single word being spoken. For instance, leaning slightly forward when someone is speaking shows interest and attentiveness, while crossed arms might be perceived as defensive. Being mindful of these cues in yourself and reading them in others can provide deep insights into the unspoken elements of communication. It helps you connect more intuitively, which can be particularly useful in navigating complex social landscapes. By aligning your non-verbal communication with your verbal interactions, you create a coherent message that resonates more effectively with those around you.

Mastering the art of reading the room means harmonizing your style with the environment without losing your unique voice. It's about observing, adapting, and respecting—skills that not only enhance your social interactions but also deepen your relationships. As you continue to practice these skills, you'll find that each social setting offers a unique opportunity to learn, grow, and connect in meaningful ways.

4.3 BRIDGING GENERATION GAPS: COMMUNICATING ACROSS AGES

Navigating the intricate dance of inter-generational communication often feels like trying to tune into different radio frequencies, where each generation broadcasts its own distinct flavour of ideas and values. Understanding this dynamic is crucial, not just for harmony at family reunions but also in multi-generational workplaces where diverse age groups must collaborate effectively. Each generation, from Boomers to Gen Z, has grown up in unique socio-economic climates, influenced by different technologies, political events, and cultural shifts, which shape their communication preferences and worldviews. For instance, while Baby Boomers may value direct and personal communication, millennials and Gen Z might prefer digital interactions, valuing speed and convenience. Recognizing these preferences is the first step in fostering effective communication across age groups. It's about appreciating where each person is coming from, what influences their perspective, and how they prefer to express themselves. This foundational understanding paves the way for more respectful and effective exchanges where everyone feels heard and valued.

Practical communication techniques can serve as valuable tools in bridging these generational divides. Consider adapting not just what you say but how you say it to resonate with different age groups. For instance, when engaging with older generations, you might opt for more formal language and perhaps more detailed explanations in face-to-face settings. In contrast, communicating with younger cohorts might involve more informal, concise messaging, often through digital platforms like emails or instant messaging apps, which they might find more engaging. Furthermore, when it involves instructions or feedback, clarity becomes paramount. Older generations might appreciate a thorough, step-by-step approach, whereas younger folks might prefer a quick, bullet-point style that allows them to dive right in. Another effective technique is to encourage mentorship in both directions, often termed 'reverse mentoring.' Here, younger employees can share their tech-savviness and fresh perspectives with older colleagues, who, in return, can share their wealth of experience and industry insights. This exchange improves communication and builds mutual respect and learning opportunities.

Addressing common misunderstandings that arise from generational differences requires patience and a proactive approach. Misunderstandings often occur when assumptions are made about a person's capability or preferences based on their age. For instance, it's a common pitfall to assume that older workers are not tech-savvy or that younger employees lack professional seriousness. To combat these stereotypes, create opportunities for different generations to collaborate on projects or share their insights in team meetings. This not only helps clear up misunderstandings but also highlights the unique strengths each age group brings to the table. Regular feedback sessions can also help address ongoing issues before they escalate, ensuring all voices are heard, and any miscommunications are swiftly and effectively resolved.

Embracing the value of diverse age perspectives can significantly enrich personal interactions and workplace culture. Each generation brings a unique set of skills, experiences, and ideas that, when harnessed effectively, can lead to innovative solutions and a more dynamic environment. For example, older generations might bring a depth of industry knowledge and a knack for strategic thinking. In comparison, younger generations might bring fresh ideas and proficiency with new technologies. Celebrating these contributions can foster an atmosphere of inclusion and collaboration. Encourage the sharing of knowledge across generations, perhaps through organized' knowledge exchange' workshops or informal 'storytelling' sessions where team members from different generations share their experiences and professional journeys. This not only helps bridge the generational gap but also cultivates a culture of continuous learning and mutual respect.

As you navigate the rich tapestry of inter-generational communication, remember that each interaction is an opportunity to learn from each other, to challenge our preconceptions, and to build stronger, more connected relationships. Whether it's adapting your communication style, addressing misunderstandings, or leveraging the diverse perspectives different generations offer, each step is a step towards creating a more inclusive and harmonious environment. So, next time you find yourself frustrated or misunderstood across the generational divide, take a moment to tune into their frequency, and you might just find a whole new world of perspectives opening up before you.

4.4 OVERCOMING SOCIAL ANXIETY WITH PRACTICAL STRATEGIES

When it comes to social interactions, it's not uncommon to feel like you're on a rollercoaster—ups of anticipation and excitement, followed by downs of anxiety and nervousness. For many, social anxiety isn't just a fleeting pre-party jitters but a persistent shadow that can cloud even the smallest interactions. Understanding the triggers of social anxiety is like being handed a map in a dense forest—it doesn't remove the trees, but it helps you navigate through them more confidently. For you, it might be walking into a room full of strangers or speaking up in a meeting. These triggers generally stem from a fear of judgment or not living up to one's own or others' expectations. Start by identifying your personal triggers. Keep a small journal or notes in your phone detailing instances when you felt anxious and what you think might have sparked those feelings. Recognizing these patterns is your first step toward managing them effectively, not by avoiding these situations but by preparing yourself to face them with greater resilience.

Breathing and grounding techniques can be powerful tools to help manage the physical symptoms of anxiety. These methods work by shifting your body's response from 'fight or flight' to 'rest and digest,' a more relaxed state where social interactions seem less daunting. One effective technique is the 4-7-8 breathing method, where you breathe in deeply for 4 seconds, hold the breath for 7 seconds, and exhale slowly for 8 seconds. This controlled breathing helps decrease your heart rate and brings your nervous system back to equilibrium. Another grounding technique involves sensory awareness, where you focus on your immediate environment and name five things you can see, four you can touch, three you can hear, two you can smell, and one you can taste. This practice helps pull your mind away from anxiety and anchors it in the present moment, reducing overwhelming feelings and helping you stay centred and focused.

Building social confidence is not unlike building muscle—it requires regular exercise and, sometimes, stepping out of your comfort zone. Start with small, manageable steps. For instance, if speaking in public is a trigger, you might begin by speaking up more in smaller group settings or with friends. Set small weekly goals, like initiating a conversation with a colleague or asking questions during a meeting. Celebrate these small victories—they are signs of your growing confidence. Over time, gradually increase the complexity of these interactions. This incremental approach not only builds your social confidence but also minimizes the risk of overwhelming yourself. Remember, the goal here is consistent progress, not an overnight transformation.

Seeking support plays a crucial role in managing social anxiety. Sometimes, the journey can get too daunting to walk alone, and there's absolutely no shame in seeking help. This could be in the form of therapy, where professionals can guide you through techniques and strategies to manage anxiety, or support groups, where you can meet others who understand what you're going through. These platforms provide not only support but also a sense of community and belonging, which are vital in overcoming feelings of isolation often associated with anxiety. Don't hesitate to reach out to a therapist who specializes in anxiety disorders or look for groups in your community or online that focus on social anxiety. Remember, asking for help is a sign of strength, not weakness, and it's a critical step towards reclaiming your confidence in social settings.

In navigating the complexities of social interactions with anxiety, remember that each step you take, no matter how small, is a step towards a more confident and composed you. Whether it's through understanding triggers, practising breathing techniques, building confidence through gradual exposure, or seeking professional help, each strategy offers a unique tool in your kit to combat social anxiety. As you continue to apply these strategies, you may find that what once seemed daunting now feels more within your control, allowing you to engage more freely and fully in the social world around you.

4.5 THE ETIQUETTE OF INTRODUCTIONS AND FAREWELLS

Navigating the delicate dance of introductions and farewells can sometimes feel like trying to remember the steps to a waltz you once watched at a wedding. You know making a graceful impression is important, but the specifics might be a bit fuzzy. Let's clear up that fuzziness and focus on the fine art of introducing yourself and others, making memorable first impressions, and parting ways in a manner that ensures you stay connected long after the initial encounter.

When you introduce yourself or make introductions in social and professional settings, think of it as laying down the welcome mat at the door of a potential new relationship. It's your chance to make everyone feel at ease, valued, and ready to connect. Start with a smile—it's the universal welcome sign. Say your name clearly, and when introducing others, ensure you pronounce their names correctly—a small effort that speaks volumes about your attention to detail and respect. If you're in a professional setting, include a brief, relevant piece of information about the person you're introducing, like their role or a recent accomplishment. For instance, "This is Jenna, our project manager, who just led us through a successful product launch last week." This not only breaks the ice but also gives a starting point for conversation. In social settings, find a common interest or connection, "Tom, meet Clara; you both have a passion for vintage cars!" Such tidbits can spark conversation, making the introduction more engaging and memorable.

Making a positive first impression is about more than dressing well or having a firm handshake—it's about conveying warmth, confidence, and competence from the start. Your body language plays a crucial role here. Stand tall, maintain eye contact, and keep your body open and facing the other person, showing that you're fully engaged and present. Be attentive and listen actively. People often appreciate and remember how attentive you were more than the words you exchanged. In these moments, you're not just sharing information about yourself; you're also signalling your interest in building a relationship, whether it's by nodding in agreement, laughing at a joke, or commenting thoughtfully on what the other person says.

Now, let's talk about the art of saying goodbye in a way that ensures you leave as good an impression as when you arrived. Whether you're wrapping up a casual coffee chat or a formal meeting, how you say goodbye can determine whether the door you're closing is locked or left open for future interactions. Make your farewells warm and personal. A simple "I really enjoyed our conversation" or "Thank you for sharing your insights; I learned a lot" can leave a lasting positive impression. Ensure you use the person's name, "It was great meeting you, Alex," which adds a personal touch that people appreciate. If it's a professional setting and you want to keep the door open for future interactions, express your intent to stay in touch, "Let's connect over LinkedIn," or "I'll send you that article we talked about by tomorrow." This not only sets the stage for future communications but also shows that you value the connection and are proactive about maintaining it.

Lastly, follow-up etiquette is what separates fleeting interactions from blossoming relationships. It's about reinforcing the connection made during your initial meeting. Send a follow-up email or message within 24 to 48 hours of your meeting—it shows you're interested and engaged. Keep it brief, personalize it with details from your conversation, and express your appreciation for the time spent together. If you promised any follow-up actions, like sending information or making an introduction, be sure to deliver on those promises promptly. This builds trust and shows your integrity. If it's a new personal connection, a message saying, "I had a great time! Let's catch up again soon." can keep the newly formed bond warm. These small gestures make a big difference in how your relationships evolve, turning introductions and farewells into gateways for deeper connections.

4.6 NETWORKING: CREATING OPPORTUNITIES THROUGH EFFECTIVE COMMUNICATION

In the vast ocean of career opportunities, networking is the sail that helps you navigate toward your next big break or collaboration. Think of networking as a skill and an essential personal asset in today's interconnected world. Whether you're attending a bustling conference or a more intimate professional gathering, having a strategy in place can transform your networking from aimless mingling to targeted, fruitful interactions. Begin with a clear objective: what are you hoping to achieve? Are you looking for a job, seeking advice, or scouting for potential business partners? This clarity will not only give you a sense of purpose but will also help you identify the right events to attend and the right people to connect with. Once at the event, instead of trying to meet everyone, focus on making a few meaningful connections. Quality here triumphs over quantity. Engage in conversations where there's mutual interest and where you feel you can genuinely offer something of value, be it your expertise, your company's services, or even just an enthusiastic ear.

Crafting an elevator pitch is like writing a mini-advertisement about yourself—one that is concise, engaging, and memorable. This brief introduction is your chance to make a compelling first impression. It should succinctly communicate who you are, what you do, and what you're looking for. Tailor it to spark interest and invite further conversation. For example, instead of saying, "I'm a marketing executive," you could say, "I help companies tell their story in a way that resonates with their audience and drives sales." Notice how the latter provides a hook and opens the door for a deeper dialogue about your skills and experiences. Practice your pitch until it feels natural. Deliver it confidently and with an open smile, ensuring it invites interaction rather than sounding like a rehearsed monologue.

Building authentic connections is the heart of effective networking. It's about fostering relationships that are based on genuine interest and mutual benefit rather than seeing people as mere stepping stones to your next career move. Approach each conversation with the mindset of how you can help the other person. Listen attentively, ask insightful questions, and show that you're interested in more than what they can do for you. This authenticity is often reciprocated, leading to stronger, more meaningful professional relationships. Remember, networking is a two-way street; it's about building bridges, not just climbing ladders. When you focus on genuine interactions, you create a network that's not only broad but also supportive and engaged.

Maintaining professional relationships over time is where many falter, but it's crucial for nurturing a robust network. Consistency is key. Keep in touch through occasional check-ins via email or social media. Share updates or articles you think might interest them, or simply drop a note to congratulate them on a recent accomplishment. These small gestures keep the relationship warm and show that you value the connection beyond the initial interaction.

Additionally, make an effort to meet up when possible, be it at professional events or more informal settings. These face-to-face interactions can strengthen bonds and reaffirm your commitment to the relationship. Remember, a well-maintained network is a powerful asset; it can open doors, provide support during career transitions, and offer insights and opportunities that might not be accessible otherwise.

In wrapping up this exploration into effective networking, remember that each interaction and connection is a thread in the larger fabric of your professional journey. By approaching networking with a strategic mindset, crafting a memorable elevator pitch, building authentic relationships, and diligently maintaining these connections, you enrich your career prospects and professional experience. These efforts ensure that your network remains a dynamic and supportive element of your career, continually opening doors and fostering growth.

As we close this chapter on mastering social interactions, we've equipped ourselves with the tools not just to survive but to thrive in the social aspects of our professional lives. From making impactful small talk to navigating complex generational dynamics, overcoming social anxiety, and mastering the art of networking, each skill contributes to a more robust, more effective professional presence. Let's carry these insights forward as we continue building and nurturing the relationships that shape our careers and lives. Now, let us turn the page and delve into the next chapter, where we explore the nuances of professional communication, further enhancing our ability to make a mark in our respective fields.

BECOME AN AMBASSADOR FOR EFFECTIVE COMMUNICATION

"Nothing in life is more important than the ability to communicate effectively."

— GERALD R. FORD

Communication is at the heart of everything we do as humans, and we spend most of our time doing it, whether we realize it or not. It stands to reason that it plays such an important role in realizing success in both our personal and professional lives, and there's no one out there who couldn't benefit from honing their skills. We can always improve, and even with all these skills under your belt, you'll continue to grow and develop your abilities with every interaction you have.

I've seen time and time again how powerful good communication skills are, and the more I've witnessed it, the more determined I've become to help others with theirs. While it may not have been the primary focus of my career, I've always taken every opportunity I could to mentor others in this field because I know how much difference it makes. This book is really just an extension of that, and my goal is to reach as many people as possible so that they can harness the power of good communication both at home and in the workplace.

Now that we're this far through our journey together, I'd like to ask for your help. There's no better person to help a new reader connect with a book than someone who has already read it and begun to put its advice into action, so simply by leaving a short review, you could make a huge difference to someone else on their quest to become a better communicator.

By leaving a review of this book on Amazon, you'll make it easy for new readers to find it, and you'll inspire them to sharpen their communication skills just as you're doing.

Communication is important in everything we do, and each one of us can benefit from improving our skills. Many people know this, and they're looking for guidance—your review will help them to find it.

Thank you so much for your support. You're making a huge difference.

Scan the QR code below

ENHANCING WORKPLACE COMMUNICATION

E ver walked into a meeting room, buzzing with the static of unspoken ideas and half-formed thoughts, only to see them evaporate into thin air the moment the session starts? As a leader, your ability to channel this latent energy into clear, actionable insights can turn the usual humdrum of meetings into a symphony of collaboration and innovation. This chapter is your guide to mastering the language of leadership, ensuring your communications not only convey information but inspire and motivate those around you. Let's decode the nuances of effective leadership communication, transforming you from just another manager into a visionary leader who speaks in a way that resonates deeply and drives your team toward excellence.

5.1 THE LANGUAGE OF LEADERSHIP: COMMUNICATING AS A LEADER

Vision Communication: Conveying your vision effectively to inspire and motivate teams

Imagine standing at the helm of a ship, the vast ocean ahead brimming with possibilities and challenges. Your team looks to you for direction and assurance—how do you communicate your vision not just to navigate but to inspire them towards uncharted territories? The art of vision communication is less about issuing commands and more about painting a picture so vivid that your team can't help but see their part in it. Start with clarity; your vision should be as clear as your favourite movie scene. For instance, if your vision is to revolutionise the customer service experience, you could describe it as a journey from a crowded, noisy airport to a serene, efficient train station. Use metaphors and analogies that resonate—think of Martin Luther King Jr.'s "I Have a Dream" speech. He didn't just state facts; he told a story, painted a picture, and touched hearts. That's your aim. Next, connect this vision to the everyday tasks of your team members. Show them how their contributions are crucial to the bigger picture, making their daily work meaningful. This connection not only boosts morale but also enhances productivity as everyone feels they are part of something larger than themselves.

Feedback and Recognition: Balancing constructive feedback with positive recognition to foster a productive work environment

Feedback is the breakfast of champions, but let's admit it: not all feedback tastes great. Balancing constructive criticism with positive recognition is like crafting a gourmet meal that's both nutritious and delicious. Start with the positive—highlight what's working well. It's not just about buttering them up before the bitter pill of criticism. Genuine praise sets a positive tone and shows that you value their efforts. Then, ease into the areas that need improvement, focusing on the behaviour or outcome, not the person. Use phrases like "Here's what could be even better" rather than "Here's what you did wrong." And always, always end on a positive note, reinforcing their ability to grow and improve. This sandwich approach ensures your feedback is digested in the spirit of growth, not as a side dish of resentment.

Decision-Making Discussions: Facilitating open discussions to involve team input in decision-making processes

Imagine your team as a jazz band. Each member plays a unique instrument, contributing to the overall harmony. As a leader, think of yourself as the conductor. Your role in decision-making discussions is to encourage each member to play their part, ensuring that the final melody is richer for it. Facilitate these sessions by setting the stage for open, honest dialogue. Pose challenging questions, such as 'What are the potential risks of this decision?' or 'How can we ensure everyone's voice is heard in this process? ', then step back and let the discussions unfold. Encourage quieter members to voice their thoughts by directly asking for their input, showing that every opinion matters. When team members feel their voices are heard in decision-making, they're more committed to the outcome, turning routine compliance into active engagement. This inclusive approach not only leads to better decisions, as you benefit from diverse perspectives but also strengthens team cohesion.

Crisis Communication: Maintaining calm and clear communication during crisis situations to guide and reassure your team

Crisis situations are the true test of leadership. The storm hits, the winds howl, and all eyes are on you. How you communicate during these times can either send your team into a tailspin or rally them to pull together like never before. Start with transparency—share what you know, what you don't, and what you're doing to find out. This honesty builds trust and prevents the rumour mill from churning out monsters. Keep your messages clear and concise, avoiding jargon that might muddy the waters.

And most importantly, communicate with empathy. Recognise the stress and anxiety your team may be feeling. A leader who shows genuine care and determination can turn fear into resolve, guiding their team through the storm with a calm, steady hand.

5.2 TEAM DYNAMICS: FACILITATING EFFECTIVE GROUP COMMUNICATION

When you think about your team, imagine it as a complex, dynamic ecosystem—each member is a unique species contributing to the habitat's balance. To cultivate a thriving work environment, foundational trust is as critical as sunlight is to a forest. Now, how do you cultivate this trust? It all starts with transparency and consistency in your communication. Imagine you're consistently open about team goals, individual roles, and the reasons behind key decisions. This openness acts like sunlight piercing through a dense canopy, reaching every layer of the forest floor. It helps clear up the underbrush of doubts and fears that can choke productivity. Moreover, consistency in your communication is like the reliable seasons that guide the forest's life cycles. When team members know what to expect and when, it stabilises the environment, allowing them to focus on growth and contribution rather than survival.

Conflict in a team is as natural as thunderstorms are to this forest ecosystem—while they can be intense and even a little bit frightening, they are also vital for clearing the air and nurturing new growth. The key to managing these storms lies not in avoidance but in how you handle them. Effective conflict resolution techniques are your tools for keeping the soil fertile and the flora healthy. Start by fostering an atmosphere where team members feel safe to express dissenting opinions without fear of repercussions—a space where conflicts are viewed as opportunities for learning rather than battlegrounds. As a leader, your role in this is to actively encourage diverse viewpoints, ensure that all voices are heard, and model respectful disagreement. When a dispute arises, approach it with a mediator's mindset: listen impartially, validate each standpoint, and then guide the discussion towards a solution that benefits the whole ecosystem, not just one or two flamboyant species. By resolving conflicts in a way that strengthens team cohesion, you're essentially enriching the soil, making it robust enough to support new ideas and relationships.

In any vibrant ecosystem, biodiversity is a strength—the variety of plants and animals enriches the habitat, making it resilient and adaptable. The same goes for your team. Encouraging diverse perspectives is about valuing this biodiversity and recognizing that each unique viewpoint adds depth and strength to the team's collective output. Create an environment that not only accepts but seeks out and values different opinions. Encourage team members from various backgrounds to share their unique insights and show genuine interest and appreciation for these new ideas. It's about cultivating a culture where diversity is seen as a treasure trove of potential waiting to be explored. This could involve structured brainstorming sessions where everyone is given a voice or informal coffee chats to celebrate and explore cultural differences and unique experiences. By nurturing this diversity, you're not just decorating your ecosystem with exotic flowers; you're building a forest resilient in the face of challenges, capable of producing rich, varied fruits.

Finally, think of regular check-ins and updates as the water cycle of your ecosystem—essential for sustaining life, maintaining alignment, and building momentum. These regular interactions ensure that everyone is nourished with the information they need to thrive. Set a rhythm for these check-ins, be it weekly one-on-ones, bi-weekly team meetings, or monthly all-hands sessions. Use these opportunities not just to track progress but to celebrate milestones, address concerns, and realign activities with overall goals. This consistent rhythm keeps the team connected, engaged, and unified towards shared objectives. It's like rain nurturing the forest—too little and things dry out, becoming brittle and lifeless; too much and the environment becomes swampy, bogging down movement. Finding the right frequency and format for these updates will keep your team's roots healthy and their growth vigorous.

By weaving these strategies into the fabric of your team dynamics, you transform your work environment from a mere collection of individuals into a thriving, productive ecosystem. This approach not only enhances daily work life but fosters a robust, dynamic, and harmoniously effective team.

5.3 NAVIGATING DIFFICULT CONVERSATIONS AT WORK

Preparation and Mindset: Approaching difficult conversations with the right preparation and mindset

Picture this: you're about to have that chat. You know the one—where you need to address something tricky, maybe a performance issue, a sensitive feedback session, or even negotiating a conflict between team members. The butterflies in your stomach are more like frantic birds. But here's the thing: with the right preparation and mindset, you can transform those flutters into a performance worthy of a seasoned conductor leading a symphony through a complex score. First, your preparation should be thorough. Gather all the facts, understand the history, and know the outcomes you hope to achieve. This isn't about scripting every moment but about being clear on your objectives. Next, check your mindset at the door. Approach the conversation with the intention to understand and resolve, not to win. Think of yourself as a detective, not a prosecutor. This shift in perspective reduces defensiveness on both sides and opens up a dialogue that is more about finding solutions than assigning blame. Remember, your role here is crucial—you set the tone, and with the proper preparation, you're paving the way for a constructive exchange.

Structuring the Conversation: Frameworks for structuring conversations to ensure clarity and constructive outcomes

Now, let's talk structure because even the best improvisers need a tune to play. Structuring your conversation is like creating a map for a road trip. Without it, you might end up going in circles or, worse, off a cliff. Start with a clear, open-ended question to break the ice and signal that this is a dialogue, not an interrogation. Something like, "Can you share your perspective on how the project is going?" This invites the other person to open up and sets a collaborative tone. As you move into the heart of the conversation, focus on the issue, not the person. Use "I" statements to express your concerns without casting blame. For example, "I've noticed the deadlines slipping, and I'm concerned about how we can realign on the project timelines." This approach keeps the conversation objective and focused. Ensure to actively listen, paraphrasing what you've heard to confirm understanding. As you wrap up, summarize the key points, agree on the next steps, and express confidence in the ability to move forward together. This framework not only keeps the conversation on track but ensures both parties leave with a clear understanding of the discussion and a roadmap for resolution.

Emotional Intelligence: Leveraging emotional intelligence to navigate sensitivities and maintain professionalism

Emotional intelligence is your secret weapon here. It's what lets you read the room, understand the undercurrents, and respond not just to words but to the emotions behind them. When navigating sensitive topics, tune into your own emotional state and that of the other person. Are they anxious, defensive, or perhaps feeling unheard? Acknowledge these emotions without judgment. Say something like, "I can see this isn't easy, and I really appreciate you discussing it with me." This kind of empathetic engagement helps de-escalate emotions and demonstrates your commitment to a respectful and constructive dialogue.

Additionally, manage your own responses. Keep your emotions in check to maintain professionalism. If the conversation gets heated, don't hesitate to suggest a brief pause, allowing everyone a moment to regroup. Remember, the goal is to solve a problem, not amplify it. By staying emotionally aware and responsive, you navigate these conversations with tact and grace, preserving relationships even when tackling tough issues.

Post-Conversation Follow-Up: Effective follow-up strategies to ensure resolutions are implemented and relationships maintained

Think of the end of the conversation not as a full stop but as a comma, leading into the next chapter of action and ongoing engagement. Effective follow-up is crucial—it's what separates a promising talk from actual progress. After a difficult conversation, summarise the agreed actions in a follow-up email, providing a written record for both parties. This isn't just about keeping track but demonstrating your commitment to moving forward. Set specific check-ins to discuss the progress made on the agreed-upon actions. These aren't just about accountability but are opportunities to provide support and recognition for efforts made. It's also wise to keep an open line for feedback. Encourage the other person to share how they feel things are going post-conversation. This helps catch any ongoing issues early and strengthens the trust and openness in your professional relationship. Through thoughtful follow-up, you ensure that the solutions found are effectively implemented and that the professional bonds are not just maintained but strengthened, paving the way for a collaborative and supportive work environment.

5.4 EMAIL ETIQUETTE: CRAFTING CLEAR AND PROFESSIONAL MESSAGES

Imagine your email as your ambassador, marching into the inboxes of colleagues, clients, and bosses, waving your flag. The way this ambassador speaks, dresses, and delivers your message can either open doors or gently close them with a polite 'we'll get back to you' that never comes. Let's ensure your emails are heard and welcomed with open arms, starting with the all-important subject line. Think of the subject line as the headline of your newspaper article. It should grab attention for all the right reasons, indicating clearly what the email is about and its level of urgency. If you're sending a monthly report, a simple "Monthly Performance Report - September 2023" is clear and direct. If something needs immediate attention, phrases like "Urgent: Response Needed by EOD" work wonders. This clarity helps recipients prioritize their responses and manage their inbox effectively, ensuring your message isn't lost in the digital shuffle.

Now, about the tone of your email. Striking the perfect balance between professional and approachable can some-times feel like threading a needle while riding a rollercoaster. Here's a little secret: matching the tone to your relationship with the recipient and the context of your message can make this much easier. For instance, an email to a long-standing client with whom you have a friendly relationship might include a light, warm opening, like "Hope you're gearing up for a great weekend!" However, first-time communication with a senior executive should be more formal with respect to hierarchies and initial boundaries. Regardless of the tone, ensure your message remains respectful and professional. This approachability doesn't just make reading your email a pleasant experience; it also fosters positive relationships, making collaborators and colleagues more likely to engage with you willingly and openly.

Structuring your message for easy reading and action is next. In our fast-paced world, no one has the time to sift through a jungle of text, hoping to stumble upon the hidden treasure of your point. Break your email into short paragraphs with clear subheadings if needed. Start with a brief introduction, setting the stage for what's to come. Follow with the body where you dive into the details—keep this focused and concise. Use bullet points to list important aspects or actions needed. Conclude with a clear call-to-action telling the recipient what you expect them to do next, be it a reply, a task completion, or a confirmation. This structure respects the reader's time and increases the likelihood of your email achieving its objectives.

Lastly, let's talk about attachments and follow-ups. If you're attaching files, mention them in the body of your email to avoid the all-too-common oversight where recipients miss the attachments. A simple "Please see the attached file for detailed figures" does the trick. As for follow-ups, they are essential but should be timed and executed tactfully. No one appreciates being hounded with daily "Just following up!" emails. If your email requires urgent action, state the deadline in the initial email and follow up a day before the deadline if you've yet to receive a response. For less urgent matters, a follow-up a week later is reasonable. This strategy ensures you stay on the radar without becoming an annoyance, maintaining professionalism and respect in all your email interactions.

Navigating email etiquette is about more than just following rules. It's about communicating in a way that respects both the message and the recipient, ensuring that your communications are as effective and welcoming as possible. Whether you are clarifying a project timeline or congratulating a team on a job well done, these guidelines help ensure that your emails are crafted with clarity, respect, and professionalism, making each one a positive reflection of you and your work ethic.

5.5 PRESENTING WITH CONFIDENCE: TIPS FOR IMPACTFUL PUBLIC SPEAKING

When you step up to the podium, it's not just about delivering a message; it's about commanding a presence, engaging your audience, and leaving a lasting impression. Picture yourself not merely as a speaker but as a conductor orchestrating an experience. The first step to this high-level performance begins long before you actually speak—it starts with a deep dive into understanding who's in your audience. What are their professional backgrounds? What might their expectations be from your talk? Are they industry veterans hungry for detailed insights or newcomers eager for basic concepts? Tailoring your message to fit your audience's specific interests and knowledge levels ensures that your content resonates well and keeps engagement high. Think of it as customizing your playlist to fit the vibe of a party; when the tunes match the crowd's taste, the night is a hit.

Let's talk about structure because even the most thrilling stories fall flat without a good framework. Organizing your content should be like planning a journey — there's a starting point, significant landmarks, and a destination. Begin with a hook, something that grabs attention right out of the gate—be it a startling statistic, a provocative question, or a relevant anecdote. This sets the tone and piques curiosity. From there, map out your main points like stepping stones guiding your audience through the narrative. Each point should build on the last, creating a cohesive flow that naturally leads to your conclusion. Here, clarity is king. Avoid cluttering your path with too much technical jargon or meandering side-tracks. Keep your landmarks clear and your paths well-marked. And when you reach your destination—the conclusion—make sure it's impactful. Reinforce your key message, and if possible, end with a call to action that inspires your audience to think, change, or act.

Moving from what to say to how to say it, your delivery can make or break your presentation. This is where your verbal and non-verbal skills shine. Maintain a confident yet approachable tone, varying your pitch to keep the auditory landscape interesting—nobody enjoys a monotone drone. Pace your delivery to allow key points to sink in, using pauses effectively; they give your audience time to digest information and give you a moment to gather your thoughts. Eye contact helps forge a connection with your audience, making your delivery feel personal and engaging. Remember also to use your hands; gestures can emphasise points and aid in expressing enthusiasm. However, like spices in cooking, use them wisely—too little may be bland, too much overwhelming. Practising these elements in front of a mirror or with friends can help you refine your delivery style until it feels natural and effective.

Handling Q&A sessions with aplomb is the final touch in mastering public speaking. This part of your presentation is unpredictable, but it's where you can truly connect with your audience. Always listen carefully to each question, showing genuine interest and respect for the questioner. If a question is complex, don't hesitate to clarify it before answering to ensure you're addressing what was truly asked. Keep your responses concise and focused, resisting the urge to digress into less relevant areas. If you encounter a question for which you don't have an answer, admit it candidly but consider offering to find out the information and follow up. This honesty can enhance your credibility and shows that you value accurate and reliable information over pretending expertise. Lastly, managing this session with a calm demeanour and a friendly smile will encourage more audience interaction and make the experience enjoyable for both you and your listeners.

In mastering these elements of public speaking, from understanding your audience to structuring your content, delivering it effectively, and managing interactions, you equip yourself not just to speak but to resonate. Each presentation becomes an opportunity to not only share knowledge but to inspire and connect with others on a level that transcends mere words.

5.6 VIRTUAL MEETINGS: ENGAGING AND EFFECTIVE ONLINE COMMUNICATION

Imagine you're setting up the stage for a big theatre production. Every light, every microphone, every backdrop is crucial to ensure the show goes off without a hitch. Similar attention to detail is vital when preparing for virtual meetings, which have become the new boardrooms of our digital era. First things first, ensure your technology is up to par. This means checking your internet connectivity, ensuring your video conferencing software is updated, and your audio and video gear work seamlessly. Think of it as the tech rehearsal before the main event. Set up in a quiet, well-lit room where interruptions are minimised. This helps reduce distractions and projects a professional image that can often be diluted in virtual settings. Encourage your team to do the same, perhaps even sharing a quick checklist of setup essentials before each meeting. This preparation stage sets the tone for professionalism and ensures that the focus remains on the content of the meeting, not on technical difficulties.

Engaging an audience in a virtual setting can be quite the magic trick. Without the physical cues and energy of in-person interactions, virtual meetings can sometimes become passive, one-way information streams. To keep the magic alive:

1. Employ interactive strategies that foster participation.
2. Use the chat function to conduct real-time polls or to ask for questions and comments throughout the session.

3. Introduce small group breakouts using virtual breakout rooms, which can re-energize participants and encourage more personal interaction.

Another effective technique is to call on participants by name for their input or to share their experiences related to the discussion at hand. This not only keeps everyone on their toes but also adds a personal touch, making the virtual space feel more connected. Remember, the goal is to mimic the dynamism of face-to-face meetings as closely as possible, making everyone feel involved and invested in the conversation.

In the realm of virtual meetings, visual aids and collaboration tools are your best allies. They can transform a monotonous monologue into an engaging, interactive dialogue. Utilise slide presentations, infographics, or live screenshares to illustrate your points vividly. These tools help in breaking down complex information and keep the audience visually engaged. Additionally, collaborative platforms like digital whiteboards where participants can add their notes or shared documents where they can co-edit are fantastic for brainstorming sessions and collaborative tasks. They not only make the meeting more interactive but also enhance the feeling of teamwork, which is crucial for maintaining a cohesive team dynamic in a virtual environment.

Lastly, the importance of recording meetings and documenting key takeaways cannot be overstated. In a virtual setting, where information can sometimes be missed due to connectivity issues or distractions at home, having a recorded session that participants can refer to later is invaluable. It ensures that no critical information is lost and that everyone is on the same page post-meeting. After the meeting, take the time to summarise the key points discussed, action items agreed upon, and any decisions made. Share this summary with all participants, ensuring clarity and accountability. This practice not only helps reinforce the topics discussed but also keeps the team aligned on the next steps, driving productivity even after the meeting ends.

As we wrap up this chapter on enhancing workplace communication, remember that whether it's through the sharp clarity of your emails, the persuasive power of your presentations, or the inclusive dynamics of your virtual meetings, every communication you undertake plays a pivotal role in shaping your professional landscape. These strategies are not just about making you a better communicator but about enriching your professional interactions, making every meeting, every email, and every presentation an opportunity to foster stronger, more effective collaborations. Now, let's turn the page and explore how these communication skills play out in more specialized scenarios, ensuring you're equipped to handle even the most niche situations with finesse.

BUILDING A PROFESSIONAL BRAND THROUGH COMMUNICATION

I magine your professional brand as your personal signature. This unique mark encapsulates your identity, values, and expertise in a world crowded with standard fonts. How you communicate, both online and offline, becomes the ink with which this signature is written. It's not just about what you say; it's about how you say it, when you say it, and to whom you say it. This chapter is dedicated to helping you craft and convey your professional narrative that reflects your authentic self and strategically enhances your presence in your industry.

6.1 STORYTELLING YOUR WAY TO SUCCESS: THE NARRATIVE OF YOUR PROFESSIONAL JOURNEY

Identifying Your Story: Crafting a compelling narrative that highlights your unique journey and strengths

Let's begin with the foundation of your professional brand: your story. Think about those pivotal moments in your career — perhaps it was the project that turned a failing company around under your leadership, or maybe it was your innovative approach that broke sales records. These aren't just points on your resume but chapters of your professional saga. To craft your narrative, start by identifying these key moments. Reflect on the challenges you faced, the strategies you employed, and the outcomes you achieved. Each of these elements showcases different facets of your professional identity — resilience, creativity, and leadership, to name a few. But here's the kicker: don't just list these achievements. Weave them into a coherent narrative that connects your past experiences with your current career aspirations. This storyline should not only highlight your skills and successes but should also give insights into your personal growth and professional evolution. It's about creating a narrative that's not only impressive but also relatable and inspiring.

Authenticity in Storytelling: Maintaining authenticity while strategically shaping your professional narrative

As you narrate your professional journey, the key is to stay genuine. Remember, the most engaging stories are those that resonate with truth and authenticity. It's tempting to embellish facts to make your story more dramatic or compelling. However, the truth has a power that no amount of embellishment can match. Authenticity builds trust, and trust is the cornerstone of all professional relationships. As you craft your narrative, be honest about your experiences and forthcoming about your failures as well as your successes. This doesn't mean focusing on the negatives; rather, it's about showing how you've learned and grown from every experience. Share the lessons learned and how they've shaped your approach and philosophy in your professional life. This not only humanizes your narrative but also enhances your credibility and relatability, fostering a sense of trust and connection with your audience.

Mediums for Your Story: Choosing the right platforms and opportunities to share your story

Choosing the right platforms to share your story is like picking the right stage for a play. Each platform has its own audience, culture, and expectations. LinkedIn, for example, is a powerful tool for professional storytelling. It allows you to share your resume and post articles, updates, and achievements, facilitating a narrative that's ongoing and dynamic. However, don't limit yourself to just online platforms. Industry conferences, networking events, and even informal meetups provide opportunities to share your story verbally.

These interactions allow for more personal engagement, often leading to meaningful professional relationships and opportunities. The key is to tailor your narrative to fit the medium and audience. A structured and polished version of your story is appropriate for more formal settings like conferences. In contrast, a networking event might call for a more casual and succinct rendition. By understanding the power of different platforms and how to leverage them, you can strategically share your story and empower your professional journey.

Impact of Storytelling: The power of storytelling in building connections and opening professional opportunities

The impact of effective storytelling in professional settings can be profound. Stories are memorable; they stick with us far longer than facts or data. Sharing your professional journey in story form not only makes it easy for others to remember you and your achievements but also inspires them to craft their own compelling narratives. Moreover, a compelling narrative can open doors to new opportunities. It can pique the interest of potential employers, attract collaborators, or even draw in clients. Think of your story as a bridge connecting your past experiences with potential future opportunities. It provides a context that enriches your professional interactions, making them more meaningful and impactful. By effectively sharing your story, you set yourself apart in a crowded market and establish a strong personal brand that resonates with authenticity and purpose.

In this digital age, where countless professionals compete for recognition and opportunities, having a clear, engaging, and authentic narrative about your professional journey is more crucial than ever. It's not just about where you've been; it's about where you're going and why others should take notice. Through strategic storytelling, you can transform your career path into a compelling narrative that captures the attention and imagination of your peers, superiors, and potential collaborators, paving the way for a professional life not just lived but also well-told.

6.2 ELEVATOR PITCHES: SELLING YOUR IDEAS SUCCINCTLY

Imagine you're in an elevator, and, surprise, you're sharing this brief ride with someone who could potentially skyrocket your career. You've got just a minute to make an impression. It sounds a bit like a plot twist in a movie, right? But here's where crafting your elevator pitch comes into play—a compact, persuasive snapshot of who you are and what you bring to the table. The core of a killer elevator pitch lies in its ability to be both concise and compelling. Start by pinpointing the essence of what you do, focusing on what sets you apart. Let's say you're a digital marketer; instead of just stating your job title, you might say, "I craft digital stories that turn brand interactions into lasting customer relationships." This not only explains what you do but also why it matters, all while hinting at your unique approach. Your pitch should also include a key achievement or statistic that underscores your expertise, such as, "I've driven a 300% increase in engagement through targeted social media strategies." This kind of data quantifies your impact and validates your expertise in a tangible way.

Tailoring your message to your audience is crucial, and it requires a keen sense of perception and adaptability. The pitch you'd deliver in a casual networking event will differ markedly from the one you'd offer in a formal investor meeting. Understanding your audience's background, their industry, and their interests allows you to highlight aspects of your work that resonate most strongly with them. For instance, if you're speaking to a potential employer in the tech industry, you might emphasize your proficiency in the latest digital marketing software and data analytics. Conversely, for a local business owner, you might focus on how your skills can drive local traffic and increase community engagement. Adjusting your pitch doesn't mean overhauling your story each time; rather, it's about shifting the focus to align with the interests and needs of your listener, making your pitch as relevant and engaging as possible.

Practising your delivery is just as important as crafting your content. Even the most compelling pitch can fall flat if delivered poorly. Start by practising in front of a mirror to monitor your body language and facial expressions—confidence is key, but so is approachability. Record yourself to hear your tone and pace; aim for a conversational yet enthusiastic tone, and be wary of speaking too fast, which is a common reflex when nervous. Get feedback from friends or mentors and pay attention to their facial expressions as they listen—are they engaged, confused, or indifferent? This feedback can be invaluable in refining your pitch. As you become more comfortable, begin to vary your delivery to keep it fresh and adaptable to different situations. The goal is for the pitch to sound natural like you're sharing a part of your story, not reciting a memorized script.

Recognising and seizing opportunities to deliver your elevator pitch can significantly enhance your professional trajectory. Always be prepared to share your pitch, whether at planned events such as industry conferences and networking meetups or in more spontaneous settings like a community workshop or even a flight. The key is to keep your pitch ready to go at a moment's notice. This readiness means keeping your pitch updated as your career evolves and as new accomplishments can be woven into your narrative. Each time you deliver your pitch, consider it a mini-performance, one that could open the door to new opportunities and deepen your professional relationships. Remember, your elevator pitch is more than just words; it's the opening line of your professional story, inviting listeners to learn more about you and potentially play a role in your career journey.

6.3 THE ART OF PERSUASION: INFLUENCING DECISIONS AND OPINIONS

Imagine sitting at a negotiation table; the stakes are high, and the tension is palpable. You're armed not just with facts and figures but with a powerful tool—persuasion. Persuasion is the subtle art of influencing others, guiding them gently towards your viewpoint without them feeling coerced. It's about crafting resonating arguments, stirring emotions, and appealing to logic in equal measure. To wield this tool effectively, it's crucial to understand the psychological principles that underpin persuasion. One such principle is the rule of reciprocity, which suggests that people are naturally inclined to return favours. When you start by offering something of value, be it a helpful insight or a meaningful concession, you're not just building goodwill but setting the stage for a reciprocal action. Another principle is the concept of commitment and consistency, where people strive to be consistent with what they have previously said or done. So, if you can get a verbal commitment at the beginning of a conversation, the chances are higher that the person will align their subsequent actions with that commitment.

But as Spider-Man's Uncle Ben famously said, "With great power comes great responsibility." This is especially true for persuasion. Ethical persuasion is rooted in respect and integrity. It's about making your case passionately but also transparently, ensuring that the facts are clear and the decisions are made with informed consent. Never manipulate or mislead. Instead, use persuasion to clarify, educate, and guide. For instance, if you're persuading your team about a new business strategy, lay out the benefits and challenges. Let them know what's in it for them and the company, and be honest about the potential hurdles. This builds trust, and trust is a cornerstone of effective persuasion. It ensures that your persuasive efforts are considered credible and considerate, not manipulative tactics.

In the practical application of persuasion, every interaction —from high-stakes negotiations to daily communications— offers an opportunity to practice and perfect this skill. In negotiations, for example, framing is key. How you present an offer can dramatically affect how it's received. Instead of saying, "We need to cut costs by 20%," try framing it as "Let's improve our efficiency to enhance profitability." The positive spin makes the pill easier to swallow and opens up creative avenues for achieving the goal.

Similarly, storytelling can be a powerful, persuasive tool during presentations. Instead of bombarding your audience with data, weave the data into a narrative that shows the real-world impact of your points. Tell the story of how your product helped clients increase their revenue or how a strategy pivot saved thousands of dollars. Stories make your points vivid and memorable, enhancing your persuasive impact.

Finally, building consensus and buy-in among teams or stakeholders is often the ultimate test of your persuasive skills. It's about aligning diverse viewpoints towards a common goal. Start by creating a shared understanding of the objective. Why is the goal important? How does it align with the broader mission of the team or organisation? Once there's agreement on the objective, facilitate open discussions that allow everyone to voice their opinions and concerns. Listen actively and acknowledge the validity of different perspectives, even if they don't align with your own. Then, gently guide the conversation towards potential solutions that incorporate varying viewpoints. The aim is to create a sense of shared ownership of the final decision. This makes the implementation smoother and ensures that the decision is supported by a strong, united team ready to pull in the same direction.

Through understanding the principles of persuasion, practicing ethical persuasion, applying these techniques in everyday scenarios, and mastering the art of consensus-building, you enhance your ability to influence outcomes positively. These skills empower you to navigate the professional landscape more effectively, making you a valued leader, a respected negotiator, and a trusted colleague.

6.4 CREATING A POSITIVE DIGITAL FOOTPRINT THROUGH THOUGHTFUL COMMUNICATION

In the vast, interconnected web of digital communications, every tweet, post, and update is like a digital brushstroke on the canvas of your professional image. Picture your online presence as a garden—you want it to be lush, inviting, and reflective of your expertise, not overgrown with weeds or neglected. The key to cultivating this garden begins with your online professional profiles, particularly on platforms like LinkedIn. These profiles are often the first point of contact between you and potential employers, clients, or collaborators. To maximize their impact, consider your LinkedIn profile your digital handshake—firm, professional, and friendly. Ensure your photo is current and professional, as this is often the first element that captures attention. Your headline shouldn't just state your job title but also hint at your major professional strengths or values. For example, instead of "Marketing Director," try "Strategic Marketing Director with a passion for building powerful brands." This gives viewers a snapshot of what you do and how you approach your profession. Dive deeper into your summary section; this is your chance to tell your story in a nutshell, highlighting your achievements, skills, and even a bit of your personality. Remember, while keywords are important for searchability, the human touch will make your profile stand out.

Shifting from profiles to content creation, you can really start to sow the seeds of your expertise across the digital landscape. Content creation is not just about broadcasting your knowledge; it's about contributing valuable insights that engage and benefit your community. Start a blog, create videos, or post articles that reflect not only what you know but also what you think. What trends are you excited about? What lessons have you learned the hard way? What unique perspectives do you bring to your field? For instance, if you're in digital marketing, sharing case studies from your latest campaign or insights on the latest SEO trends showcases your expertise and helps others. Remember, the goal here is to provide value, which in turn enhances your professional stature. Engage with your audience by asking questions or inviting feedback to make your content a two-way conversation rather than a monologue.

Engaging with your network is like watering this digital garden. It's not enough to just connect with others; nurturing these connections with regular, meaningful interactions can turn them into thriving professional relationships. Make it a habit to comment on posts by your connections, offering genuine insights or encouragement. Share their content with your network, adding your thoughtful commentary, which not only amplifies their message but also shows you as an engaged and supportive professional. Reach out with personalized messages on occasions like job changes or birthdays. These small gestures make a big difference in maintaining a warm, active presence within your network. They keep you on the radar of your connections, increasing the likelihood of opportunities coming your way through referrals or direct offers.

Monitoring and managing your digital footprint is crucial in maintaining the health of this garden. Just as you wouldn't want weeds overtaking your garden, you also wouldn't want inappropriate or outdated content tarnishing your professional image. Use tools like Google Alerts to track where your name or content appears online. Regularly review your social media profiles and content to ensure they align with the professional image you want to project. Are there posts that no longer reflect your views or position? It might be time to prune. Also, consider tightening your privacy settings on personal accounts to control what's visible to the public. This not only helps in managing what others see about you but also protects you from potential digital mishaps that could affect your professional reputation.

By nurturing your digital footprint with thoughtful communication and regular engagement, you create a vibrant, flourishing presence that attracts opportunities and showcases your professional capabilities. This isn't just about being visible; it's about being impactful, turning every digital interaction into a stepping stone towards greater professional achievements.

6.5 FEEDBACK AS A TOOL FOR GROWTH: ENGAGING IN CONSTRUCTIVE EXCHANGES

Let's talk about feedback, not just as a formality in your annual reviews but as a golden opportunity for growth and connection. Imagine feedback as a compass that guides your professional journey, pointing you towards areas for improvement and reaffirming the paths you've navigated well. Soliciting feedback effectively is akin to inviting someone into your personal workspace and asking them to help you rearrange the furniture for better flow. You want to encourage honest and constructive responses that really make a difference. Start by being specific about the feedback you seek. Instead of a broad "How am I doing?" try "What could I have done to make that presentation more impactful?" This makes it easier for others to provide focused insights and shows your commitment to specific growth areas. Furthermore, create a safe space for feedback by expressing your openness and gratitude for any insights shared. It's about setting the stage where others feel their opinions are valued and taken seriously, not just heard as a formality.

Receiving feedback is where many of us hit a roadblock. It's like hearing a recording of your voice; it can be cringe-inducing even though it's essential for improvement. The key here is to cultivate a mindset where feedback is viewed as a valuable input, not a personal critique. When receiving feedback, practice active listening—nod, maintain eye contact, and resist the urge to interrupt or defend yourself. This shows respect and helps you absorb the information more effectively. After receiving feedback, reflect on it. Ask yourself how it aligns with your self-perception and your professional goals. Sometimes, the feedback may require you to pivot or embrace new methods. Other times, it might reinforce that you're on the right track but need minor adjustments. Remember, each piece of feedback is a stepping stone to a more refined version of your professional self.

Giving feedback, on the other hand, is an art form in itself. It's about delivering insights in a digestible and empowering way, not discouraging. Begin by highlighting strengths. It's like applying a soothing balm before addressing a wound. Point out what's working well to reinforce positive behaviours. Then, when addressing areas for improvement, use the 'situation-behavior-impact' model. Describe the situation, outline the behaviour, and discuss its impact. For instance, instead of saying, "Your report was unclear," you could say, "In the team meeting yesterday, when you presented the report, some key points were not fully detailed, which left a few team members confused about their next steps." This not only makes your feedback specific and actionable but also depersonalizes it, focusing on the behaviour and its outcomes rather than on the person. Wrap up the feedback session with suggestions for improvement and an offer to assist. This shows your commitment to helping the individual grow and turns the feedback into a constructive conversation rather than a critique session.

Creating a feedback culture within your workplace transforms occasional feedback into a regular, valued practice. It's about embedding feedback into the daily rhythms of your team interactions, making it as natural as morning coffees. Encourage regular 'feedback exchanges' where team members can share insights in a structured yet informal setting. Recognize and reward those who actively participate and use feedback constructively, whether through verbal acknowledgements in meetings or more formal recognition systems. This not only incentivizes engagement but also gradually weaves feedback into the fabric of your team's culture. Over time, this culture of open, constructive feedback can drive innovation, enhance collaboration, and significantly boost team morale and productivity. It turns feedback from a feared encounter into a welcomed opportunity for personal and professional development, fostering an environment where growth is part of the daily agenda and every team member feels valued and understood.

6.6 CULTIVATING A CULTURE OF OPENNESS AND INNOVATION THROUGH COMMUNICATION

Establishing channels that encourage open communication and idea-sharing is like setting up a grand stage for a festival of ideas within your workplace. It's where every voice gets a microphone, and every concept gets a spotlight, however raw or refined it may be. Imagine transforming your office environment in such a way that dialogue flows freely, barriers are dismantled, and every team member feels empowered to voice their thoughts without hesitation. This can be achieved through regular open forums or innovation hubs where individuals from different departments can come together to brainstorm and share ideas. Digital tools like internal collaboration platforms can also be instrumental in this process, allowing for continuous sharing and development of ideas. The key here is accessibility; ensure that these channels are easy to use and that everyone feels comfortable using them. This kind of openness not only nurtures a thriving culture of communication but also sparks creativity, as people feel more relaxed and engaged in an environment that values their input.

Encouraging innovation through communication is about fostering an environment where creative problem-solving is not just welcomed but actively encouraged. Start by celebrating out-of-the-box thinking; when someone comes up with a novel idea, recognise their creativity publicly. This recognition can be as simple as a shout-out in a team meeting or as formal as an innovation award. It sends a powerful message that creative thinking is valued and desired. Additionally, provide team members with tools and resources to experiment and prototype their innovative ideas safely and with the necessary support. Workshops or seminars on creative thinking and problem-solving can also be very beneficial. These initiatives help to equip your team with the skills to think differently and tackle problems from new angles, fostering a culture where innovation is part of the daily conversation.

Recognizing and rewarding contributions effectively is crucial in maintaining motivation and commitment to innovation. It's about acknowledging both the successes and the effort. Implementing a rewards system that appreciates not just the big wins but also the small steps forward can significantly enhance morale and drive. Consider incorporating peer recognition programs where team members can nominate each other for awards. These programs boost morale and enhance team cohesion as everyone sees the collaborative spirit being celebrated.

Moreover, ensure that these rewards are meaningful. Beyond traditional bonuses or certificates, consider rewards that truly resonate with your team's values and needs, like additional creative time, professional development opportunities, or team outings. By aligning rewards with your team's preferences and values, the recognition feels more personal and motivating.

Promoting a mindset where failures are seen as opportunities for learning and growth can transform the way your team approaches challenges and risks. It's about shifting the narrative from a fear of failure to a culture that questions, 'What can we learn?' When projects don't go as planned, instead of zeroing in on the mishaps, lead discussions that explore what the experience taught the team. Conduct 'retrospective' meetings to discuss not only what went wrong but also what went right and what could be improved for next time. Encourage team members to share their experiences and insights openly and ensure that these conversations are constructive, focusing on solutions and learning rather than blame. This approach alleviates the fear of failure and empowers your team to take calculated risks, knowing that the learnings gleaned from the outcomes are valued and will lead to personal and professional growth.

In wrapping up this exploration into fostering a culture of openness and innovation, remember that the goal is to create an environment where communication flows freely, ideas are celebrated, failures are seen as springboards for growth, and contributions are recognised and rewarded. By embedding these practices into your workplace culture, you not only enhance the innovative capacity of your team but also build a strong, cohesive, and resilient organisation. Now, let's move forward to the next chapter, where we will delve into advanced communication strategies that will further refine your skills and expand your professional influence.

NAVIGATING THE DIGITAL AGE
OF COMMUNICATION

Think of the digital world as a bustling city square. It's where news travels fast, where ideas meet and mingle, and where your digital persona can either flourish like a well-tended garden or wither like an unwatered houseplant. Navigating this digital square requires a certain savoir-faire, especially when it comes to wielding the double-edged sword of social media. Here, authenticity clashes with curation, personal brands are built in tweets and posts, and the digital trolls lurk under the bridge of every comment section. Ready to become a social media savant? Let's dive into the art of communicating authentically online, building a resilient brand, engaging positively, and gracefully handling the inevitable digital downers.

7.1 SOCIAL MEDIA SAVVY: COMMUNICATING AUTHENTICALLY ONLINE

Authenticity vs. Curation: Balancing genuine self-expression with the curated nature of social media

In the glossy world of social media, it's easy to fall into the trap of presenting only the highlight reels of our lives and careers—perfectly polished posts that shimmer with success. But here's the twist: while a curated feed can attract attention, it's the raw, relatable posts that build deeper connections. Imagine sharing not just your triumphs but also your trials, not in a bid for sympathy but as a way to say, "Hey, I'm human, just like you." This doesn't mean airing personal grievances or oversharing; rather, it's about finding a balance. Share your successes, by all means, but also talk about the hurdles you've overcome to get there. This blend of authenticity with thoughtful curation fosters a genuine connection with your audience, turning casual followers into loyal fans.

Building Your Brand: Using social media to build a personal or professional brand with integrity

Your social media profiles are more than just digital platforms; they are the building blocks of your personal or professional brand. Each post, like, and comment is a brushstroke in the portrait you present to the online world. To paint a picture that resonates with authenticity and professionalism, start by defining the core values that you want your brand to embody. Are you all about creativity, resilience, innovation, or perhaps a mix of all three? Once these cornerstones are set, let them guide your online behaviour. Share content that reflects these values, engage with others in a manner that reinforces them, and create a narrative that weaves your values into every story you tell. This intentional and strategic approach to branding ensures that your online activities are purposeful and align with your professional goals, making your social media presence a reliable landmark in the ever-changing digital landscape.

Engagement Strategies: Effective ways to engage with your audience and foster meaningful interactions

Engagement is the currency of the social media realm. It's not just about broadcasting your message into the digital void but about sparking conversations and building a community. Start with the basics: respond to comments, messages, and questions promptly and thoughtfully. But why stop there? Go further by initiating discussions, asking your audience for their opinions or experiences, and creating content that invites interaction, like polls or question-based posts. Host live sessions where you can interact in real-time, offering a behind-the-scenes look at your work or a Q&A session. These strategies boost your engagement rates and make your followers feel connected, valued, and seen, transforming passive viewers into active participants in your digital narrative.

Navigating Trolls and Negativity: Strategies for dealing with negative interactions in a healthy and professional manner.

Ah, the trolls! No journey through the digital woods is complete without encountering these creatures. They thrive on provocation, hiding behind screens to disrupt and distress. Here's how to handle them: first, take a deep breath. Responding in haste can escalate the situation. Evaluate whether the comment merits a response—if it's constructive criticism, engage politely and use it as an opportunity to show your professionalism. If it's outright trolling, consider ignoring or, if necessary, blocking the user. Remember, your digital space is your domain, and you set the rules. Maintaining a professional demeanour, setting clear boundaries, and knowing when to disengage are key strategies for managing the darker side of digital interactions. This approach helps keep your digital garden a place of growth and positivity, not a battleground for online altercations.

Navigating the digital landscape requires a blend of authenticity, strategic branding, engaged communication, and savvy handling of negativity. By mastering these skills, you enhance your digital presence and build a brand that stands out for its integrity and genuine connection with its audience. Now, let's continue exploring the digital realm, ensuring that every tweet, post, and share contributes positively to your professional journey.

7.2 THE DOS AND DON'TS OF TEXTING AND MESSAGING IN PROFESSIONAL CONTEXTS

When it comes to texting and instant messaging in the professional realm, think of it as walking a tightrope; you need just the right balance of brevity and formality, friendliness, and professionalism. Starting with the basics, professional texting etiquette is not just about what you say but how and when you say it. Imagine you're texting a colleague or a client—this isn't the time for "Hey, what's up?" or "Yo!" Instead, opt for a polite opener, even something as simple as "Hi [Name], I hope you're well." It sets a respectful tone right from the get-go. Always use full sentences and check your grammar. Text speak, abbreviations, and a casual tone can come across as unprofessional or, worse, unclear. You want your message to be as crisp as a freshly ironed shirt. And remember, the sign-off matters too; a simple "Thank you" or "Best regards" can do wonders to maintain the professional sheen of your communications.

Navigating the urgency and response times in professional texting is another critical aspect. Let's say your boss texts you after hours. The ping might make your heart race a bit—do you need to respond immediately, or can it wait until morning? Here's a rule of thumb: if it's during work hours and the matter is urgent, respond as soon as possible, preferably within the hour. If it's after hours, assess the urgency. If it's truly urgent, a prompt response shows your commitment and reliability. However, if it's not pressing, responding during the next working day is generally acceptable. This helps manage your work-life balance and sets healthy boundaries with your colleagues and clients.

Emojis and informality have their place in professional texting. Still, it's a bit like adding chilli to a dish—not everyone will appreciate the extra spice. Use emojis judiciously and choose ones that are universally understood and appropriate for professional contexts, like a simple smiley :) Or a thumbs up 👍. They can soften the tone, convey friendliness, and sometimes help clarify the emotional intent behind your words, reducing misunderstandings. However, remember the context and the recipient. If you're messaging someone for the first time or it's a more formal business relationship, you might want to keep the emojis in the drawer until you better understand the other person's communication style.

Finally, let's talk about privacy and confidentiality, the twin guardians of professional integrity in digital communications. In an era where data breaches are just a hack away, ensuring the confidentiality of your professional texts and messages is paramount. Always be cautious about sharing sensitive information over text or instant messaging apps. If you must share something confidential, make sure it's through secure, encrypted platforms that your organization approves. Additionally, be mindful of where and how you store these messages. Leaving sensitive information unattended on your phone or computer can be like leaving your house keys in the door—it might be fine, but it's a risk you shouldn't take.

Navigating the nuances of professional texting and messaging requires a blend of good judgment, awareness of digital etiquette, and an understanding of the technological tools at your disposal. By mastering these elements, you ensure that your digital communications are effective, efficient, secure, and respectful of professional boundaries and personal privacy. As you continue to text and message within your professional circles, keep these guidelines in mind to maintain a polished, professional digital persona.

7.3 MANAGING DIGITAL MISCOMMUNICATIONS AND CONFLICTS

In the digital realm, where tone can be as elusive as a clear sky in London, misunderstandings and conflicts are more common than we'd hope. Picture this: you dash off a quick email thinking your message is as clear as day, only to find it's sparked a storm in a teacup because the receiver interpreted your tone as terse or dismissive. It's like stepping on a digital landmine—you don't see it until it explodes. Preventing such mishaps requires finesse and a toolkit of clarification techniques designed to defuse tensions and clarify intentions without escalating the situation further.

Let's start with the art of clarification. When a misunderstanding occurs, the key is to address it promptly and clearly. Suppose you send a message saying, "Please address this issue by tomorrow," and it's interpreted as you being unnecessarily pushy. To clarify, you could follow up with, "Apologies if my previous message seemed rushed. I meant to emphasize the urgency from the client's end. Let's touch base to discuss how we can tackle this together." This approach clears up the misunderstanding and reinforces teamwork and shared goals. It's about turning potential conflict into a collaborative effort to meet a common challenge. In digital communications, where the warmth of face-to-face interaction is absent, such clarifications are vital in maintaining harmony and clear lines of communication.

Moving on to resolving conflicts that arise in digital settings, the landscape here requires a navigational strategy that combines tact with transparency. Online conflicts, whether in email threads or social media platforms, can escalate quickly due to the public nature of these exchanges and the permanence of the digital footprint. The best practice here is to take the conversation offline or to a more private channel as soon as you realize the conflict is deepening. A simple "I see this is an important issue. Let's schedule a call to discuss this in detail and find a solution" can shift the exchange to a more controlled and less emotionally charged environment. During the resolution process, focus on understanding the other party's perspective and expressing your points without placing blame, using "I" statements instead of "you" to communicate your thoughts and feelings about the situation, not the person's character.

Tone misinterpretations are another minefield in digital communications. Without the benefit of vocal inflexions or facial expressions, even a well-intentioned message can come across as cold or aggressive. To navigate this, pepper your communications with phrases that explicitly convey your emotional tone. For instance, expressions like "I'm really looking forward to your thoughts on this!" or "I hope this message finds you well" can set a positive, collaborative tone. Also, consider the medium—texts or instant messages can feel more casual and may allow for a lighter tone. At the same time, emails might require a more formal approach depending on the context and your relationship with the recipient. Being mindful of these nuances can help prevent the kind of misunderstandings that lead to conflicts in the first place.

Lastly, knowing how to apologize and correct mistakes gracefully is crucial when missteps occur, and they inevitably will. Digital apologies should be as thoughtful as their offline counterparts. Acknowledge the mistake clearly, take responsibility without making excuses and state how you intend to correct or address the issue. For example, if an incorrect report was emailed, a follow-up might be, "I realized I sent you the preliminary report by mistake, and I apologize for any confusion. I am attaching the correct final report here. Thank you for your understanding and patience." This shows professionalism and reinforces your integrity and commitment to accountability.

Navigating digital communications with the skill of a seasoned diplomat can enhance your professional relationships, build trust, and maintain a positive online presence. By employing these strategies, you ensure that your digital interactions are as clear, respectful, and constructive as possible, turning potential digital pitfalls into platforms for professional growth and collaboration.

7.4 EMAIL VS. IN-PERSON VS. PHONE: CHOOSING THE RIGHT MEDIUM

Navigating the maze of modern communication can sometimes feel like choosing the right outfit for a surprise party—

you want to strike just the right note, appropriate yet adaptable. Whether to drop an email, make a phone call, or arrange a face-to-face meeting can dramatically influence the effectiveness of your message and the response it elicits. Let's unfold the intricacies of selecting the most fitting medium to ensure your message not only lands but resonates.

Imagine you're about to deliver some delicate feedback to a team member. An email might give you the space to choose your words carefully, but it lacks the warmth and immediate interactivity of voice or facial expressions, which can often mitigate the sting of criticism. Here, a phone call or an in-person chat can add a personal touch, allowing you to modulate your tone and respond in real time to the other person's reactions, softening the blow and ensuring your feedback is constructive rather than crushing. On the other hand, if you're confirming meeting details or providing a quick update, an email serves as a tangible reference point that both parties can refer back to, reducing the possibility of miscommunication over times and venues that more informal chats might entail.

Each medium carries its arsenal of advantages and limitations. Email is fantastic for creating a record of exchanges and is less disruptive than a phone call, allowing the recipient to respond at a time that suits their workflow. However, its Achilles' heel is the coldness of text-based communication, where nuances can be lost and messages misinterpreted. Phone calls provide immediate interaction and the warmth of human voice, facilitating quick clarifications and fostering rapport. Yet, they lack the visual aids of emails or face-to-face meetings, which can be crucial when discussing complex information. In-person meetings, the gold standard for detailed discussions and sensitive negotiations, offer the full spectrum of verbal and non-verbal communication. Still, they require scheduling and travel that isn't always practical or necessary.

Choosing the right medium often hinges on the context of the message. If timeliness and clarity are paramount, an email might be your best bet. If the situation calls for negotiation or you aim to build a relationship, picking up the phone or scheduling a coffee might yield better results. It's about matching the medium to the message's priorities—urgency, complexity, and personal touch.

Transitioning smoothly between these mediums is an art form in itself. You could start with an email proposal, follow up with a phone call to iron out details, and seal the deal with a personal meeting. This fluid movement between communication forms can keep interactions dynamic and effective, adapting to the evolving needs of the conversation. For instance, after a project briefing via email, a quick phone call can ensure all parties are clear on their roles and responsibilities, providing an opportunity for immediate questions and clarifications that ensure everyone is on the same page.

Navigating these choices adeptly requires a keen sense of timing, a clear understanding of your communication goals, and a good read on the preferences and expectations of those you're communicating with. As you make these decisions, consider not just what you need to convey but also how it can best be received, ensuring your message not only delivers but also engages.

7.5 DIGITAL NETWORKING: MAKING GENUINE CONNECTIONS ONLINE

Imagine the digital landscape as a vibrant marketplace, where every tweet, post, and share is a handshake, an introduction, or a business card exchange. In this bustling environment, platforms like LinkedIn become not just tools, but lifelines to thriving professional networks that can propel your career forward. To truly leverage these platforms, think beyond just collecting connections like baseball cards. It's about cultivating relationships that are as real and valuable online as they would be if you were face-to-face at a networking event. Start by optimizing your profile to serve as your digital handshake. Ensure it's not just complete but compelling—rich with details that showcase your skills, experiences, and, most importantly, what makes you a valuable connection. Engage actively and thoughtfully with your connections' content. Comment with insightful observations or supportive feedback, and share posts that align with your professional values and interests. This kind of genuine interaction is key in transforming a name on a screen into a meaningful part of your professional circle.

Now, let's talk about virtual networking events and webinars, the digital equivalent of conferences and business meetups. These platforms offer a unique opportunity to expand your network beyond geographical boundaries, connecting you with professionals across the globe. To make the most of these events, preparation is your best friend. Before the event:

1. Research the speakers and the attendees, if possible.
2. Identify individuals you'd like to connect with based on shared interests or potential collaborations.
3. During the event, participate actively.
4. Ask questions during Q&A sessions, contribute to discussions, and engage in breakout rooms.

These interactions can often lead to connections that are as strong as those made in person. And don't forget the follow-up—a quick message or connection request referencing the interaction can help cement the connection and open doors to further communication.

Creating value in your connections is about more than just expanding your network; it's about enriching it. Each inter-action should add a layer of worth for you and the person on the other side of the exchange. One effective strategy is to become a resource for your connections. Share articles, tools, and resources that are relevant to your industry. Offer your expertise when someone seeks advice or post thoughtful questions that spark professional discussions. By consistently providing value, you position yourself as a knowledgeable and generous professional, someone others want to reach out to and keep on their radar. This approach enhances your reputation and attracts further valuable connections, creating a virtuous cycle of professional growth and opportunity.

Maintaining online relationships over time can sometimes feel like trying to keep a plant alive in a windowless room. It requires regular attention and the right nourishment. Schedule time each week to check in on your digital network. Congratulate connections on their professional achievements, share relevant information, or simply drop a note to catch up. Utilize features like LinkedIn's reminders about work anniversaries or birthdays as prompts for reaching out. These small gestures keep the relationship vibrant and ongoing, preventing your network from becoming a list of names you barely remember. Additionally, consider organizing or participating in regular virtual catch-ups or webinars that can help maintain and deepen these connections. By nurturing these digital relationships with consistent and meaningful interactions, you ensure your network remains a dynamic and supportive element of your professional life, growing and evolving with your career.

In this digital age, where technology has blurred the lines between personal and professional lives, mastering the art of digital networking is more crucial than ever. By leveraging professional networks, making the most of virtual events, creating value, and maintaining relationships, you equip yourself with the tools not just to survive but to thrive in the digital marketplace. Each connection and each interaction becomes a stepping stone towards a richer, more connected professional journey. As you continue to navigate this digital terrain, remember that the essence of networking hasn't changed; it's about people connecting with people. The platform is just the medium, but the human connection, that's the message.

7.6 PRIVACY AND DISCRETION IN DIGITAL COMMUNICATION

In our digital age, every click, every post, and every conversation leaves a trail—a digital footprint that can be as enduring as stone. Understanding the permanence and reach of your digital communications is akin to knowing how loud you're talking in a crowded room. It's all about awareness. A vast, unseen audience can potentially access each piece of information you share online. Once it's out there, it's almost impossible to retract. Imagine tweeting a casual complaint about your job or a confidential detail about a project. Such tweets can not only harm your professional reputation but could also lead to more severe repercussions if sensitive information is involved. It's essential always to pause and consider the potential long-term visibility of what you share online, treating digital spaces more like a billboard on a busy highway rather than a diary under your pillow.

Diving deeper into the toolbox for maintaining digital privacy, using privacy settings on social media and communication platforms becomes crucial. Each platform offers a range of settings designed to control who sees your content and how your data is managed. For example, platforms like Facebook and LinkedIn allow you to customize the visibility of your posts and personal information. Taking the time to understand and configure these settings can protect you from unintended audiences. Moreover, tools such as two-factor authentication add an extra layer of security to your accounts, safeguarding against unauthorized access. Regular audits of your privacy settings—like checking the locks on your doors periodically—ensure they remain effective and adapted to any new features or policies the platforms might introduce.

When it comes to discretion in sharing, the mantra "think before you post" is golden. In a professional context, this discretion becomes even more critical. Guidelines for what to share and what to keep private can safeguard your professional integrity and personal privacy. Before sharing any information online, ask yourself: Is this necessary to share? Could this information be used against me or misinterpreted? Is it sensitive or confidential? Applying such filters can prevent potential professional conflicts and personal complications. For instance, sharing vacation plans publicly might inform potential burglars when your house will be empty, just as discussing client details could breach confidentiality agreements.

Legal and ethical considerations in digital communications often intertwine with privacy and discretion. Laws such as the EU's General Data Protection Regulation (GDPR) provide a framework for handling personal data, emphasizing transparency, security, and accountability. Not adhering to these laws can lead to substantial fines and damage to your professional credibility. Ethically, respecting the privacy and confidentiality of others in your digital communications is just as crucial. This includes not sharing information about others without their consent and being cautious about collecting and using data in professional settings. Understanding these legal and ethical dimensions helps you navigate the complex web of digital interactions more safely and responsibly, ensuring that your digital engagements are not only effective but also compliant and respectful of privacy norms.

As we wrap up this exploration into the delicate balance of privacy and discretion in our digital interactions, remember that the digital realm is a public space, albeit with private corners. Navigating this space with mindfulness and informed caution can prevent missteps that might compromise your personal or professional life. Each post, each share, and each interaction in the digital world is a reflection of you, embedded in the digital landscape, sometimes indefinitely. As we move forward, keeping these principles in mind will ensure that your digital presence is impactful and protected, paving the way for safer and more effective digital communications. As we close this chapter, we look ahead to further refining our communication skills in the digital age, ensuring that each step we take online is as secure and effective as those we take in the physical world.

THE FUTURE OF COMMUNICATION

Welcome to the fascinating frontier of communication, where the lines between human interaction and technological innovation blur to create experiences straight out of science fiction. As we peer into the crystal ball of communication technologies, one titan looms large and seemingly omnipotent—Artificial Intelligence, or AI as it's fondly called. This isn't just about machines taking over mundane tasks; it's about transforming the very fabric of how we connect, converse, and convert thoughts into actions.

8.1 THE IMPACT OF ARTIFICIAL INTELLIGENCE ON COMMUNICATION

AI in Personal Assistants: How AI personal assistants are changing the way we communicate and organize our lives

Imagine waking up to a soft voice that tells you the weather and how it might affect your schedule and mood. No, it's not your partner being extra considerate; it's your AI personal assistant, seamlessly integrating into your daily life like a helpful ghost in the machine. AI assistants like Siri, Alexa, and Google Assistant are increasingly becoming our partners in crime (and productivity), managing our calendars, sending reminders, or even ordering coffee—all through conversational interfaces that mimic human interaction. The sophistication of AI in understanding and processing natural language has revolutionised our interaction with technology, turning erstwhile clunky interfaces into smooth, conversational experiences. This shift is not just about convenience; it's about creating a more intuitive and human-like interaction with technology, where you chat rather than click.

Automated Customer Service: The role of AI in transforming customer service and engagement

Now, let's turn our attention to customer service, where AI is playing a matchmaker between efficiency and personalisation. Chatbots and virtual assistants powered by AI provide 24/7 customer service, handling everything from simple queries about store hours to complex issues like troubleshooting technical problems. The beauty of AI in this domain lies in its ability to learn from interactions and improve over time, providing increasingly personalised responses. This enhances customer satisfaction and frees up human agents to handle more nuanced and complex customer needs. The result? A win-win situation where customers enjoy quick, efficient service, and businesses streamline operations and boost satisfaction, all wrapped up in the cost-effective bow of AI technology.

Ethical Considerations: Examining the ethical implications of AI in communication, including privacy concerns

With great power comes great responsibility, and AI is no exception. The increasing reliance on AI for personal and professional communication brings to light significant ethical considerations, particularly concerning privacy. As AI systems process vast amounts of personal data to learn and adapt, the potential for misuse or breach becomes a stark reality. Ensuring that AI systems respect user privacy and data security is not just a technical challenge but a moral imperative. Strict ethical standards must guide the development and deployment of AI in communication to protect user data and ensure transparency in how this data is used. As we integrate AI more deeply into our lives, maintaining this ethical compass is crucial to fostering trust and acceptance among users.

Future Potential: Speculating on future advancements in AI that could further revolutionise communication

Looking ahead, the horizon is aglow with potential AI innovations that could further transform communication. Imagine AI systems that can detect and adapt to emotional nuances in human speech, providing responses that are not just contextually appropriate but also emotionally resonant. Or consider the possibility of AI-driven translation services that allow real-time, seamless conversation between individuals speaking different languages, breaking down language barriers like mere curtains rather than concrete walls. The future could also see AI contributing to social good, such as developing communication aids for those with speech or hearing impairments, thus broadening the scope of 'normal' communication. As AI continues to evolve, its potential to enhance, enrich, and expand human communication is bound only by the limits of our imagination—and perhaps a bit of robust ethical coding.

As we navigate this brave new world of AI-driven communication, it's clear that the future is not just about technology; it's about how we harness this technology to foster clearer, more meaningful connections. Whether it's through your trusty AI assistant or a customer service bot, each interaction is a step toward a future where technology understands us a little better, making our world a little smaller and a lot more connected.

8.2 VIRTUAL REALITY: THE NEXT FRONTIER IN PERSONAL AND PROFESSIONAL INTERACTION

Immersive Communication: The potential of VR to create immersive and interactive communication experiences

Step into a world where your morning meeting happens on a virtual beach, complete with the soothing sound of waves and a panoramic ocean view. No, it's not a holiday—this is the power of virtual reality (VR) transforming your typical workday interaction. VR's capacity to create deeply immersive environments is not just about dazzling visuals; it's about crafting experiences that engage all senses, fostering a level of interaction that traditional video calls or in-person meetings can seldom match. Imagine discussing a new product design with your team, where instead of looking at flat images, you can walk around a life-sized 3D model, examining every angle together despite being continents apart. This level of immersion can elevate understanding and engagement, making collaborations more productive and enjoyable. The emotional resonance of VR environments also plays a crucial role in communication. Being in a calming virtual space can reduce meeting anxiety, promote open dialogue, and spark creativity. As VR technology continues to evolve, the potential for creating communication experiences that are not just informative but also emotionally and sensorally rich is expanding, promising a future where VR meetings could become a preferred mode of professional interaction for their ability to mimic and enhance real-world dynamics.

Virtual Meetings and Workspaces: How VR could transform remote work and virtual meetings

As remote work becomes more common, VR stands poised to revolutionise the way we perceive virtual offices. Gone are the days of static, grid-view meetings. With VR, remote workspaces can be dynamic virtual environments that mimic the layout of a real office. This setup not only enhances the sense of presence and participation but also reinstates some of the informal networking that is a casualty of remote work —like those serendipitous corridor conversations that often lead to brilliant ideas or crucial collaborations. Furthermore, VR can be programmed to support various work modes. For instance, a 'focus room' in VR could minimise external distractions, providing an ideal environment for deep work, while a 'collaboration hub' could facilitate interactive workshops and brainstorming sessions. These tailored environments can help manage workplace stress and enhance productivity by aligning the virtual space with the nature of the task at hand. As more organisations embrace a distributed workforce, VR could become essential in bridging the gap between the flexibility of remote work and the engagement of physical office spaces, offering a balanced environment where creativity and connectivity flourish.

Education and Training: The use of VR in education and training for more engaging and effective learning experiences

Imagine learning history by walking through a virtual recreation of ancient Rome or understanding complex scientific concepts by experiencing them at a molecular level—this is the potential of VR in education and training. VR's ability to simulate real-world scenarios offers learners a hands-on experience without the associated risks or resource constraints. VR provides a safe, scalable alternative for industries like healthcare, aviation, and manufacturing, where practical training is crucial but often logistically challenging or hazardous. Trainees can perform surgeries, pilot aircraft, or operate heavy machinery in a controlled, virtual setting, gaining valuable practical experience before they ever touch the real thing. Moreover, VR can cater to various learning styles and paces, making learning more personalised and accessible. For instance, visual learners can benefit from the 3D modelling of abstract concepts, while kinesthetic learners can engage in interactive simulations. This adaptability enhances learning outcomes and makes the learning process more inclusive and engaging.

Challenges and Limitations: Addressing the current limitations and challenges facing VR in communication

Despite its vast potential, VR technology is not without its challenges. The cost of VR hardware and the technical know-how required to create or operate VR environments are significant barriers to widespread adoption. Additionally, the physical discomfort—often referred to as VR sickness—associated with prolonged use of VR headsets is a real concern that needs addressing to make VR a viable option for routine communication. Moreover, there's the issue of VR accessibility. Ensuring that people with disabilities can fully engage with VR content requires thoughtful design and technological innovation to adapt user interfaces and experiences to a broad range of needs. Lastly, the psychological impacts of spending extensive periods in virtual environments are still under scrutiny. As we navigate these challenges, the focus must remain on developing VR solutions that are not only technologically advanced but also socially and ethically responsible, ensuring that the virtual worlds we create are safe, inclusive, and beneficial for all users.

8.3 THE EVOLUTION OF LANGUAGE IN THE DIGITAL ERA

Digital Linguistics: How digital communication platforms are influencing language and linguistics

Have you ever noticed how chatting online has slowly morphed how we speak and write? It's not just about slinging slang or LOL-ing. The shift is deeper, almost seismic, in how digital platforms reshape our linguistic landscape. Messaging apps, social media, and even email have forged a new dialect, a blend of brevity, emojis, and hyperlinks, each carrying its own weight in our digital conversations. This new digital dialect is dynamic, evolving constantly as we humans adapt to the ever-changing digital ecosystem. It's a fascinating dance between traditional language structures and the digital environment's demands, where clarity, speed, and expression are paramount. For instance, the art of crafting a perfect tweet or a snappy text message often involves choosing words that deliver maximum impact with minimum real estate. This digital economy of language challenges us to think more critically about word choice and sentence structure, making us sharper communicators in both digital and face-to-face contexts.

Interestingly, this shift also includes a more playful engagement with language through puns, neologisms, and playful abbreviations that enrich our interactions and make the digital sphere an exciting space for linguistic creativity. As digital natives, many of us are bilingual in this sense, seamlessly switching between more formal language in professional emails and a more relaxed, innovative digital lingo in texts or tweets. This duality showcases our adaptability and enriches our overall communication skills.

Emoji and Memes: The role of visual language, such as emojis and memes, in modern communication

Now, let's talk about emojis and memes—those colourful characters and catchy images that have become integral to our digital dialogues. Far from being mere adornments, these visual elements carry semantic weight and serve as a bridge across linguistic and cultural divides. Emojis, in particular, add nuance to digital communication, where tone is notoriously tricky to convey and easy to misinterpret. A well-placed smiley face can soften a directive, express solidarity, or add a playful tone, reducing ambiguity. Memes, on the other hand, are the cultural shorthand of the digital age, encapsulating complex emotions or reactions in a single, often humorous image. They are a form of digital storytelling, offering a snapshot of cultural attitudes, current events, or universal human experiences. Both emojis and memes enrich digital communication by providing quick, effective ways to express emotions and share cultural commentary. They act as the glue in our online conversations, fostering a sense of community and shared understanding in a way that words alone might not. Moreover, their widespread use highlights a shift towards a more inclusive form of communication that values emotional expression alongside textual clarity, creating a richer, more connected online world.

Language Simplification: The trend towards simplification and abbreviation in digital communications

The digital age is the age of speed, and with this need for speed comes a lean and efficient language. This isn't about dumbing down; it's about streamlining communication to fit the fast-paced, character-limited realms of digital interaction. Abbreviations like BRB (be right back) or IMO (in my opinion) and acronyms are part of this linguistic evolution, offering quick bursts of meaning that speed up communication without sacrificing clarity. This simplification extends to sentence structure and word choice, with a clear preference for shorter, more direct expressions. It's a practical adaptation to the scrolling speeds of our readers, who skim through vast amounts of information daily. However, this trend also challenges us to maintain the depth and nuance of our language. The key is finding a balance—keeping the efficiency of simplified language while ensuring that important subtleties and complexities are not lost. This balancing act is crucial not just for clear communication but for preserving the richness of our language, ensuring that while it evolves, it remains a robust tool for expression and understanding.

Preserving Language Diversity: The challenges and opportunities digital platforms present for preserving language diversity

In a world where major languages dominate digital platforms, there's a real concern about the erosion of linguistic diversity. Many smaller, regional languages find little space in the digital realm, which can lead to a gradual decline in their use and relevance. However, the digital age also presents unprecedented opportunities for the preservation and revitalization of these languages. Social media, blogs, and online forums offer platforms for speakers of minority languages to create content, engage in dialogue, and celebrate their linguistic heritage. Furthermore, digital technology can aid in developing language-learning apps and resources that make it easier for new generations to learn and continue using their ancestral tongues. Efforts like these help preserve linguistic diversity and enrich the global digital landscape, ensuring it reflects the true plurality of human cultures and experiences. As we continue to navigate the digital era, it's vital to leverage these technologies for global connectivity and as tools for cultural and linguistic preservation, ensuring that the voices of all communities, regardless of size or power, are heard and valued in the vast digital conversation.

8.4 GLOBALIZATION AND COMMUNICATION: BRIDGING CULTURAL DIVIDES

Cross-Cultural Communication: The importance of effective cross-cultural communication in a globalised world

In today's tapestry of global commerce and interaction, imagine each thread as a line of communication weaving through different cultures, each vibrant with its own customs, values, and modes of expression. In such a world, the ability to communicate across cultures is not just beneficial; it's imperative. Effective cross-cultural communication fosters better understanding and cooperation, whether you're negotiating a business deal in Tokyo, presenting a webinar from New York to a European audience, or coordinating humanitarian efforts across continents. It's about more than just exchanging words; it's about exchanging ideas, values, and perspectives in mutually respectful and enriching ways. The nuances of this type of communication can mean the difference between a successful international partnership and a diplomatic faux pas. For instance, while directness might be valued in some Western cultures, in many Eastern cultures, indirect communication styles are often more appropriate and respected. Navigating these differences requires an awareness of these diverse communication styles and an adaptability to switch between them as the context dictates, much like changing gears in a car depending on the terrain.

Cultural Sensitivity: Strategies for enhancing cultural sensitivity and understanding in global communications

Enhancing cultural sensitivity starts with education. Dive into the cultural backgrounds of the people you interact with —understand their history, social norms, and communication etiquette. This foundational knowledge can be a springboard for deeper engagement and more nuanced interactions. For instance, learning about the high value placed on personal honour in Arab cultures can help you understand the importance of respectful language and behaviour in business dealings. Moreover, cultural sensitivity is also about attitude—it involves a willingness to learn and sometimes to unlearn. It requires an openness to see the world from multiple perspectives and a readiness to adapt your behaviour with respect to different cultural norms. Practical strategies include:

1. Engaging in cultural sensitivity training.
2. Attending workshops.
3. Even participating in cultural exchange programs.

These initiatives can equip you with the tools to recognize and celebrate cultural differences, turning potential barriers into bridges of cooperation. Additionally, fostering a diverse workplace where multiple cultures are represented can naturally enhance cultural sensitivity, as regular interaction with colleagues from diverse backgrounds can lead to a better understanding and appreciation of different cultural perspectives.

Language Barriers: Tools and strategies for overcoming language barriers in international communication

Language barriers can be formidable, but they are not insurmountable. Technology offers a suite of tools—from real-time translation apps to multilingual customer service solutions—that can help bridge these gaps. Tools like Google Translate or Microsoft Translator can facilitate basic understanding and are continually improving in accuracy and nuance. However, professional human translators and interpreters are indispensable for situations where precision and subtlety in communication are crucial, such as legal negotiations or international conferences. Beyond technology, simple strategies like using clear, simple language (avoiding slang and idiomatic expressions that may not translate well) and confirming understanding through summaries or follow-up questions can also significantly reduce miscommunications. Additionally, learning the basics of the language of your international colleagues or clients can go a long way—not just in facilitating communication but also as a gesture of respect and goodwill. Even basic greetings or thank-you phrases can warm hearts and open doors, setting a positive tone for more effective communication.

The Role of Technology: How technology is facilitating cross-cultural communication and understanding

Technology has been a game-changer in levelling the playing field of international communication. Through collaborative platforms like Slack or Microsoft Teams, people from around the world can work together in real-time, sharing ideas and insights that transcend geographical and cultural boundaries. Video conferencing tools like Zoom or Google Meet allow for face-to-face meetings with visual cues that can help clarify meanings and enhance understanding. Social media platforms provide a space for cultural exchange and mutual learning, where diverse groups can share their stories and perspectives, enriching the global dialogue. Moreover, advancements in AI are making strides in breaking down language barriers with more sophisticated translation and interpretation solutions. These technologies are not just tools but portals to a more connected and cooperative global society where understanding and collaboration can flourish despite the diversity of languages and cultures. As we continue to innovate and integrate these technologies into our daily communication, the potential for a truly interconnected global community becomes more tangible, promising a future where cultural diversity is acknowledged and celebrated.

8.5 EMOTIONAL INTELLIGENCE IN THE AGE OF SCREENS

Digital Empathy: Developing empathy and emotional intelligence in digital communication

In the pixelated rush of likes, shares, and comments, it's easy to forget that behind every screen is a human heart, perhaps seeking connection or solace. Developing empathy in the digital realm is like trying to read emotions through a frosted glass—possible but challenging. As we navigate our digital day-to-day, incorporating emotional intelligence into our online interactions becomes beneficial and essential.

This involves tuning into the subtle cues that text-based communication offers. Phrases like "I'm fine" or "It's okay" can sometimes hide deeper feelings that would be more apparent in a face-to-face interaction through someone's tone or facial expressions. Here, empathy requires us to read between the lines—asking follow-up questions, offering support, or simply acknowledging the emotions that might lurk behind brief texts. It's about creating a digital dialogue that feels as attentive and responsive as a real-world conversation. Additionally, the use of video calls can enhance this empathetic connection, allowing us to pick up on non-verbal cues like facial expressions and body language, which are so telling of one's true feelings.

Developing digital empathy also involves being mindful of the content we share and how it might affect others. Understanding and respecting diverse perspectives and emotional responses is crucial in a world where someone across the globe can like a post. This might mean thinking twice before sharing potentially sensitive content or framing our words in ways that are considerate of a wider range of emotions and experiences. By fostering this kind of empathetic interaction, we not only enhance our own emotional intelligence but also contribute to a digital environment that prioritizes understanding and kindness over divisiveness and indifference.

Maintaining Human Connection: Strategies for maintaining genuine human connections in an increasingly digital world

As our interactions become more pixel than personal, maintaining genuine human connections can feel like holding onto a bar of soap in the bath—slippery and elusive. Yet, it's possible and profoundly rewarding. One effective strategy is prioritizing quality over quantity in our digital interactions. This means engaging in fewer, more meaningful conversations rather than spreading ourselves too thin across multiple platforms and countless threads. When we do engage, making our interactions as personal and thoughtful as possible can make all the difference. For instance, personalizing messages, recalling previous conversations, and showing genuine interest in the responses encourages a more rewarding connection.

Another vital strategy is setting boundaries around digital communication to ensure it doesn't overshadow face-to-face interactions. This might look like having 'phone-free' zones or times at home where digital devices are set aside to encourage in-person engagement with family or friends. Additionally, using technology to facilitate rather than replace personal interactions is key. Tools like video chats can supplement phone calls or texts, providing a more personal touch to long-distance communications. By consciously using digital tools to enhance rather than replace the human element, we can maintain a sense of closeness and connection, even when we are miles apart.

Screen Time and Emotional Well-Being: Exploring the impact of screen time on emotional intelligence and well-being

It's no secret that our screens can sometimes feel like both a window and a wall—connecting us to the world while isolating us from the person next to us. The impact of screen time on our emotional well-being is a complex dance of positives and negatives. On one hand, access to digital resources can support our mental health, providing tools for mindfulness, emotional regulation, and even digital therapy options. On the other hand, excessive screen time, especially on social media, can lead to comparisons, cyberbullying, and a sense of inadequacy, which can negatively affect our emotional well-being.

Balancing this requires mindful management of our screen time. Implementing regular digital detoxes—periods when we step away from our screens—can help mitigate the negative effects. During these times, engaging in activities that promote emotional well-being, such as spending time in nature, practising meditation, or enjoying hobbies, can provide a much-needed break from the digital world. Furthermore, using apps that track and manage screen time can help us become more aware of our digital habits, prompting us to make changes that align better with our emotional health. Ultimately, the goal is to cultivate a relationship with our digital devices that serves our well-being rather than detracts from it, ensuring that our screen time supports our emotional needs rather than undermining them.

Teaching Emotional Intelligence: The importance of teaching emotional intelligence skills in the digital age

As we forge into the digital future, navigating the emotional landscapes of both the real and virtual worlds becomes crucial. Teaching emotional intelligence (EI) in the digital age means equipping individuals with the skills to handle not just face-to-face interactions but also the complexities of digital communication. Schools, workplaces, and even families can play pivotal roles in fostering these skills. For instance, educational programs incorporating EI training can teach students how to manage emotions, resolve conflicts, and communicate effectively offline and online. In the workplace, EI workshops can enhance employees' ability to collaborate with colleagues, manage stress, and foster a supportive work environment.

Moreover, incorporating EI into the fabric of digital literacy —teaching individuals how to express empathy online, manage digital conflicts, and maintain digital well-being— can prepare us for a world where digital and emotional literacy are intertwined. By prioritizing the development of emotional intelligence in all spheres of life, we enhance individual well-being and interpersonal relationships and contribute to a more emotionally intelligent society where understanding and empathy extend beyond the screen and into the heart of our shared human experience.

8.6 THE ROLE OF COMMUNICATION IN SHAPING TOMORROW'S WORLD

Communication as a Catalyst for Change: How effective communication can drive social and political change

If we think about every major social shift or political wave, at the heart of each, there was a powerful piece of communication. From Martin Luther King Jr.'s "I Have a Dream" speech to the viral spread of the #MeToo movement, the right words at the right time have the power to galvanise populations and pave the way for real change. Today, with the global village more connected than ever, your voice has the potential to resonate far beyond your local coffee shop or community centre. It's about leveraging this interconnectedness to advocate for causes that matter, to shed light on injustices, and to rally communities around solutions. Picture this: every tweet you send, every blog post you publish, and every video you upload has the potential to spark thought, ignite action, and inspire change. The key is to communicate not just with clarity and passion but with a purpose. It's about crafting messages that don't just inform but also inspire, that don't just comment but also compel action. This responsibility to communicate consciously is powerful. It turns every social media user, every blogger, and every public speaker into a potential activist, a potential catalyst for change. By embracing this role, you become part of a larger narrative, a collective force pushing towards progress and equity.

The Power of Collective Action: The role of communication in organizing and mobilizing collective action

There's a unique kind of magic that happens when individuals, each with their own passions and skills, come together for a common cause. This magic, known as collective action, is significantly amplified by effective communication. Think about the last time you signed an online petition or shared a fundraiser—chances are, a compelling message convinced you to do so. Organizing and mobilizing collective action starts with the ability to communicate in ways that not only inform but also resonate on a personal level. It's about presenting the 'why' of a cause in a way that touches individual hearts, prompting not just interest but action. With their vast networks and real-time communication capabilities, social media platforms have become the town squares of the digital age. They are places where calls to action can spread like wildfire, where communities can form in support of or opposition to issues, shaping public opinion and policy at speeds previously unimaginable. But it's not just about making noise; it's about making a difference. And that difference is made through strategic, empathetic, and mobilizing communication that turns individual whispers into roars of change.

Ethical Communication: The importance of ethical communication practices in shaping a more equitable world

As the lines between digital and real-life interactions blur, the ethical implications of our communications become more pronounced. Ethical communication is rooted in truth, accuracy, fairness, and respect. It's about recognizing the power of words and using this power responsibly. In a world teeming with misinformation, where fake news can spread as fast as legitimate information, the commitment to ethical communication is more crucial than ever. It involves fact-checking before sharing, respecting privacy, acknowledging sources, and engaging in honest discourse. Ethical communication also means being mindful of the impact your words may have and striving to contribute positively to the dialogue rather than inciting division or harm. By adhering to these principles, you help foster a communication landscape that promotes truth, encourages respectful interaction, and builds community trust. This trust is the foundation upon which equitable and just societies are built. As communicators, whether through a blog post, a podcast, or a tweet, you hold the keys to this foundation. Using them responsibly means helping to shape a world where information empowers rather than misleads, where dialogue bridges gaps rather than deepening them.

Looking Ahead: Envisioning the future of communication and its potential to solve global challenges.

Imagine a future where communication has the power to not only connect us but also to heal us. A future where global challenges like climate change, inequality, and health crises are addressed not just through policies and programs but through powerful, worldwide dialogues that leverage collective intelligence and empathy. The future of communication holds limitless potential in solving these global issues. With advancing technologies and growing interconnectedness, our ability to share knowledge, inspire action, and foster global cooperation is increasing exponentially. This future is not just about speaking and being heard; it's about listening and understanding. It's about dialogue that transcends borders and barriers, about messages that mobilize resources and resolve. As we look ahead, the role of communication in shaping this promising future is undeniable. It calls for a commitment to use our voices, our platforms, and our words to not just address the symptoms but the root causes of global challenges, to not just communicate but to connect, and in doing so, to transform our world for the better.

As we close this exploration into the transformative power of communication, we touch upon the essence of what makes our interactions so potent. From being a catalyst for change to fostering ethical dialogues, the scope of communication in shaping tomorrow's world is vast and vital. As we transition to the next chapter, let's carry forward the understanding that our words are not just expressions of thought but instruments of immense power and potential. By wielding them with intention and integrity, we step into a role that is not just about sharing information but about shaping realities. Let's continue to explore, understand, and innovate in how we connect with and impact the world around us.

SHARE THE POWER OF COMMUNICATION!

In my experience, the more skilled you become at communication, the more passionate you become about sharing its power with others. This is your chance!

Simply by sharing your honest opinion of this book and a little about your own experience, you'll show new readers exactly where they can find the guidance they're looking for to help them improve their own skills.

Thank you so much for your support. You're making more of a difference than you realize.

Scan the QR code below

CONCLUSION

Well, we've been on quite the journey together, haven't we? From unravelling the intricate tapestry of human interaction to mastering the subtle art of digital dialogue, you've made significant strides. Now, as we draw the curtains on this adventure in communication, let's pause and reflect on the essential nuggets of wisdom you've gathered along the way.

First and foremost, let's reiterate the undeniable importance of effective communication. Whether you're navigating the complex dynamics of a workplace or fostering deeper connections in your personal life, the ability to communicate clearly and empathetically stands as a cornerstone of success. It's about more than just exchanging information; it's about building bridges of understanding and collaboration that can withstand the tests of time and challenge.

Through our discussions, we've revisited the foundational principles that make up the skeleton of effective communication:

1. The nuanced dance between verbal and non-verbal cues
2. The critical role of active listening
3. The transformative power of empathy

Remember, every gesture, every pause, and every listen contribute to the story you're telling.

We didn't stop at theory, though. We armed ourselves with practical strategies and exercises designed to turn knowledge into action. From overcoming those pesky communication barriers that sneak up in our daily interactions to enhancing our prowess in the digital realms and utilising storytelling to carve out a unique personal brand—these tools are your allies in the quest to communicate with confidence and clarity.

Reflecting on the transformative potential of these skills, it's clear that mastering communication can profoundly impact your personal and professional life. It's about opening doors to opportunities, fostering deeper relationships, and understanding the world—and yourself—a little better each day.

This book isn't just a collection of communication strategies; it's a blend of decades of experiences and insights from my forty-plus years in financial services, tailored to you, the career-focused, personal development-oriented adult. It's my hope that these pages serve as a practical companion in your ongoing journey of growth and self-discovery.

But remember, the path to communication mastery doesn't end here. It's a continuous journey, an art that you refine and adapt over time. Keep practising, stay curious, and embrace the learning curve. Consider diving deeper through workshops, online courses, or follow-up readings. The world is brimming with resources waiting to be explored.

I invite you to share your progress, challenges, and stories, not just keep these lessons to yourself. Reach out via social media or email, join conversations, and become part of a community that values and strives for better communication. Your experiences can inspire and enlighten others just as they can enlighten you.

And so, as we part ways in this written form, I urge you to take these lessons to heart. Use them to forge stronger connections, steer through your professional landscapes with agility, and express yourself with the authenticity and confidence that I know resides within you. Effective communication is within your reach, and it's never too late to improve how you connect with the world around you.

Go out there, communicate purposefully, and watch as doors you never noticed start opening up for you. Here's to speaking up, listening well, and connecting deeply—may these be the tools that guide you to incredible places.

Thank you for sharing this journey with me. Let the conversations begin!

REFERENCES

- *Psychology in Communication Processes* https://web.
  stanford.edu/~bailenso/papers/icae-psychology
- *Body Language and Nonverbal Communication* https://www.
  helpguide.org/articles/relationships-communication/nonverbal-
  communication.htm
- *7 Active Listening Techniques For Better Communication* https://www.
  verywellmind.com/what-is-active-listening-3024343
- *The Role of Empathy and Compassion in Conflict Resolution* https://
  journals.sagepub.com/doi/full/10.1177/1754073919838609
- *Confronting the Fear of Being Judged: A Step-by-Step Approach* https://
  www.addrc.org/confronting-the-fear-of-being-judged-a-step-by-
  step-approach/
- *5 Strategies For Cross-Cultural Communication Across Global Teams*
  https://www.forbes.com/sites/rachelwells/2023/10/03/5-
  strategies-for-cross-cultural-communication-across-global-
  teams/
- *How To Improve Articulation in 9 Steps (With Tips) | Indeed.com*
  https://www.indeed.com/career-advice/career-development/
  how-to-improve-articulation
- *10 Ways to Improve Digital Communication in the Workplace* https://
  www.lumapps.com/internal-communication/improve-digital-
  communication-workplace/
- *Why It's Important to Know Your Partner's Love Language* https://
  www.bayviewtherapy.com/single-post/why-it-s-important-to-
  know-your-partner-s-love-language
- *Family Conflict Resolution Tips and Strategies* https://www.
  verywellmind.com/family-conflict-resolution-solutions-3144540
- *Why Communicating Your Needs Is Important in Friendship* https://
  www.wellandgood.com/communicating-needs-in-friendship
- *Empathy: How to Feel and Respond to the Emotions of ...* https://www.
  helpguide.org/articles/relationships-communication/
  empathy.htm

- *The Art of Small Talk: How Casual Conversation Can Help You Network and Build Trust* https://techq.medium.com/the-art-of-small-talk-how-casual-conversation-can-help-you-network-and-build-trust-2f52fe8329e8
- *Adapting Communication Styles to Different Audiences* https://fleximize.com/articles/000592/communication-styles
- *Bridging Generational Divides in Your Workplace* https://hbr.org/2023/01/bridging-generational-divides-in-your-workplace
- *6 Ways to Overcome Social Anxiety* https://health.clevelandclinic.org/how-to-overcome-social-anxiety
- *8 Essential Leadership Communication Skills | HBS Online* https://online.hbs.edu/blog/post/leadership-communication
- *Preventing and Managing Team Conflict* https://professional.dce.harvard.edu/blog/preventing-and-managing-team-conflict/
- *How To Write a Professional Email (With Tips and Examples)* https://www.indeed.com/career-advice/career-development/how-to-write-a-professional-email
- *15 Strategies for Engaging Virtual Presentations* https://lars-sudmann.com/15-strategies-for-engaging-virtual-presentations/
- *3 Reasons Why Brand Storytelling Is The Future Of Marketing* https://www.forbes.com/sites/celinnedacosta/2019/01/31/3-reasons-why-brand-storytelling-is-the-future-of-marketing/
- *The Ethics Of Persuasion* https://www.smashingmagazine.com/2018/06/ethics-of-persuasion/
- *How To Manage Your Digital Footprint in 2024: 20 Tips for ...* https://research.com/education/how-to-manage-digital-footprint
- *8 Practical Tips For Effective Communication on Social Media* https://sumankher.com/2016/03/20/8-tips-for-better-communication-on-social-media/
- *20 Rules of Texting Etiquette for Employees* https://www.contactmonkey.com/blog/business-texting-etiquette-rules
- *Tried-and-True Tips for Minimizing Digital Conflict in the Workplace* https://trainingmag.com/tried-and-true-tips-for-minimizing-digital-conflict-in-the-workplace/
- *The Benefits Of Building Professional Networks! - LinkedIn* https://www.linkedin.com/pulse/benefits-building-professional-networks-avdgroup-
- *The Transformative Impact of AI in Communication* https://www.sprinklr.com/blog/ai-in-communications/

- *How Companies Are Using VR to Develop Employees' Soft Skills* https://hbr.org/2021/01/how-companies-are-using-vr-to-develop-employees-soft-skills
- *The Impact of Social Media on Language Evolution* https://www.linkedin.com/pulse/impact-social-media-language-evolution-siyak-consultancy-services-tn3ne
- *Emotional Intelligence in the Digital Age* https://sylviedigiusto.com/emotional-intelligence-in-the-digital-age/
- "35 Quotes About Communication to Inspire Collaboration | Vibe." Vibe: All-in-One Smart Whiteboard for Collaborative Workspace. Last modified May 5, 2022. https://vibe.us/blog/35-quotes-about-communication/

Made in the USA
Columbia, SC
10 December 2024

48698082R00093